Roman Silver Coins

By Richard

1st Edition (

INTERNATIONAL STANDARD B

A fully updated Price guide of over 850 silver Roman coins dated 280 BC - 476 AD, with their market values, notes on changes in the coinage over the years and over 700 drawings to aid identification.

CONTENTS

"Dedicated to Gabriel and Jared in memory of their grandmother Helen Leather"

www.rotographic.co.uk
0871 871 5122

Preface to this 1st Edition

This is meant to be a book for the ordinary collector, or for people just developing an interest in Roman Silver Coins. For this reason it has been made as simple as possible. Such a reader, I believe, wants to know two things about his (or her) coin; which Emperor minted it and roughly how much it is worth. On the whole the obverse portrait will, therefore, be more important than the Allegorical figure - or whatever is on the reverse. Though comparatively few reverses are catalogued, I have tried to illustrate all the obverses I have seen for Imperial coins.

The Republican period has been a headache to catalogue - I feel that the usual way of listing by family name is extremely difficult for the non-expert, so I have tried a different method. Perhaps my readers will tell me if this is any better! I am sorry that I was unable to list every Republican coin. I only hope that the selection I have offered represents most of the coins that most collectors are likely to come across.

To ease identification for those who need to thumb through the whole book to find the coin they want, I have kept the illustrations as close together as possible, and relegated descriptive notes to the end of the book. Any coin with a bold Asterisk (*****) after the value has further notes included in **Appendix I**. I have not discussed weights or purity of silver content: but I have made the illustrations as close as possible to life-sized (though size may vary between one specimen of the same coin and the next).

Important Note

In all cases the price given is for a coin in VF (Very Fine) condition. A crack across the flan, or a flan smaller than normal, or a coin being struck off-centre will very much affect the price. Plated coins will be worth much less, as will a coin which is "black" (probably through impurity of the metal).

Note also, that as one approaches 260AD and the descent of the Antoninianus into the realms of base metal coinage, a good silvered coin will be worth much more than one that is no longer well silvered.

Identification

The questionnaire on the following page is designed to help you identify your Roman Republican coins.

A coin is listed in the earliest category in which it falls. Thus **CRS178** with a ram on the reverse is listed under **GROUP 5** "Coins with notable Obverse type" not under **GROUP 6** "single animal". Unfortunately, there is a chance your coin may not be listed at all: because this is a catalogue containing the vast majority of coins that collectors will come across. It would need to be considerably larger in order to cover the vast array of all Roman Republican coins.

If your coin is not from the Republic, a full Index of both Roman Imperatorial and the Roman Empire (Imperial period) follows the questionnaire.

And if you still cannot find your coins, remember that it could be from Numidia or Mauretania in North Africa, which use Latin legends. Or, if the writing is Greek, certain coins of Caesareia in Cappadocia, of the province of Lycia, and of Amisus in Pontus can look very like Roman coins, especially when the legend is worn. It is not impossible it could even be Celtic British! Unfortunately none of these "foreigners" come within the scope of this catalogue.

Roman Republic Identification Questionnaire

Note that Groups 1 – 6 are all Denarii and usually 16 – 20mm in diameter.

Group	Description	Class	Number
	The **DIDRACHM** period before 211BC		CRS1 - 8
	From 211BC the UNNAMED coins, naming just Roma		CRS9 - 15

Are there TWO HORSEMEN or a CHARIOT on the reverse?

GROUP 1	The **DIOSCURI** (two horsemen) type		CRS16 - 49
GROUP 2	The **BIGA** (chariot pulled by two horses/other creatures)		
	Obv: Helmeted head/Reverse: Biga of horses	**Class 1**	CRS50 - 89
	Obv: Helmeted head/Reverse: Non-horse Biga	**Class 2**	CRS90 - 95
	Obv: Non-helmeted head/Reverse: Biga of horses	**Class 3**	CRS96 - 113
	Obv: Non-helmeted head/Reverse: Non-horse Biga	**Class 4**	CRS114 - 116
GROUP 3	The three-horse **TRIGA**		CRS117 - 118
GROUP 4	The **QUADRIGA** (chariot pulled by four horses)		
	Obv: Helmeted head	**Class 1**	CRS119 - 150
	Obv: Non-helmeted head, or different type	**Class 2**	CRS151 - 162

Obverse Head has a notable Head-Dress, or something unusual?

GROUP 5	Obv: Head of **ROMA**	**Class 1a**	CRS163 - 172
	Obv: Similar (but different!) helmeted head	**Class 1b**	CRS173 - 181
	Obv: Two faces on Obv, or one on Obv and one on Rev	**Class 2**	CRS182 - 188
	Obv: Front-facing head	**Class 3**	CRS189 - 190
	Obv: Heads wearing various crowns, caps, or skins	**Class 4**	CRS191 - 201

The Obverse Head has nothing remarkable about it, turn to the REVERSE:

GROUP 6	Rev: Two or more human characters/trophies	**Class 1a**	CRS202 - 214
	Rev: Two or more animals	**Class 1b**	CRS215 - 218
	Rev: Animal plus human	**Class 2**	CRS219 - 229
	Rev: Single animal	**Class 3a**	CRS230 - 239
	Rev: Single human	**Class 3b**	CRS240 - 248
	Rev: Consists entirely of inanimate objects	**Class 4**	CRS249 - 272

Is the coin less than about 16mm in diameter?

GROUP 7	The Quinarii	**Class 1**	CRS273 - 283
	The Sestertii	**Class 2**	CRS284 - 285

Alphabetical Index of Imperatorial and Imperial Coins

Alphabetical Index of Imperatorial and Imperial Coins (continued)

The DIDRACHM period before 211BC

CRS1: 280 - 276BC (Probably minted at Metapontum). Obv: Head of Mars **VF £550**

CRS2: 269 - 266BC. Obv: Hercules Rev: Wolf and twins **VF £550** *

CRS3: 265 - 242BC. Obv: Head of ?Diana or possibly ?Roma **VF £600**

CRS4: 241 - 235BC. Obv: Head of Mars **VF £650**

CRS5: 234 - 231BC. Obv: Head of Apollo **VF £550**

CRS6: 230 - 226BC. Obv: Head of Mars **VF £600**

CRS7: 225 - 212BC
Didrachm or "Quadrigatus".
Obv: "Janiform" head of Dioscuri
Rev: Jupiter in quadriga (four horse chariot)
VF £275

CRS8: 217 - 214BC
Drachm or "Half-quadrigatus".
Obv: as CRS7
VF £375

The Un-Named coins of the "Denarius" period, from 211BC

CRS9: The DENARIUS. Obv: Head of Roma. Rev: The Dioscuri (Castor & Pollux) This was tariffed at 10 asses until 123BC when it was retariffed at 16 asses.
VF £35 *

CRS10: The Half-Denarius known as the Quinarius. Rev: as CRS9
VF £50

CRS11: Sestertius (or Quarter-Denarius). Rev: as CRS9
VF £90

The Un-Named coins of the "Denarius" period from 211BC (continued)

CRS12:
The Victoriate. 211 - c170BC
Obv: Head of Jupiter. Rev: Victory crowning a trophy. Valued at 3/4 denarius. It was revived in c 101BC, becoming the model for the Quinarius (half-denarius) **VF £35 ***

CRS13a: Denarius
c189 - c170BC
Obv: Helmeted head of Roma
Rev: Diana in a biga
VF £35 *

CRS13b: Denarius
c157 - c156BC
Obv: as CRS13
Rev: Victory in a biga **VF £30**

There are just a few later un-inscribed denarii, as CRS14 and CRS15; but very soon most coins were to be named. During a transitional period some coins of Reference Numbers CRS9, CRS10, CRS12 and CRS13 began to be marked with symbols or letters and monograms. For example, CRS15a (below right) is identical to CRS9 but now has an "M based" monogram under the horses. We do not know enough about these coins to be able to attribute them to individuals. Fully named coins, however, were soon to follow.

CRS14: VF £45 *
115 - 114BC

CRS15: VF £35 *
86BC

CRS15a: VF £35
c199 - 170BC

Please note that many dates given in catalogues for this period are prefixed by 'c', meaning 'Circa', and that they are tentative! I omit the 'c', but the dates remain tentative!

The Named Coins of the Roman Republic

These begin with a large number of "Head of Roma/Dioscuri" and "Head of Roma/Chariot" coins; but later we find a wonderful variety of designs. The latter I intend to list by type, rather than alphabetically by the family name or the magistrate, as I think this will make it easier for the collector to identify a coin.

Note that 'I' and 'J' are both written as I. The 'U' and 'V' are both written as 'V'.

Note, also, that two, three, or even four letters may be tied together or "ligate".
Thus  PUR, and  ANTE

The Named Coins of the Roman Republic

GROUP 1: Coins of the "Dioscuri" type (As CRS9) with the name written, usually below the horses; but sometimes above the horse, or behind the Head of Roma on the obverse.
Values: CRS16 – 161, generally all £30 - £40 in VF. Some coins with interesting designs, or higher values, have been illustrated.

CRS18: VF £30 - £40

CRS37: VF £30 - £40

Ref	Behind Roma	Below the horses	Moneyer	Date
CRS16		CAV	C.Aelius	209-208BC
CRS17		P-PAETVS	P.Aelius Paetus	138BC
CRS18	C- ANTESTI	DOG RUNNING	C.Antestius	146BC
CRS19	DOG WALKING	C- ANTESTI	C.Antestius	146BC
CRS20	SARAN	M-ATIL	M.Atilius Saranus	148BC
CRS21		AVR	L.Autronius	189-180Bc
CRS22		TAMP (or above horse)	Cn.Baebius Tamphilus	194-190BC*
CRS23		ME	Metellus	194-190BC
CRS24		CN-CAL	Cn.Calpurnius Piso	189-180BC
CRS25		L-COIL	L.Coelius	189-180BC
CRS25a		L-CVP	L.Cupiennius	147BC
CRS26*		[illegible]	Decius	206-200BC
CRS27		CN-DO	Cn.Domitius Ahenobarbus	189-180BC
CRS28		PVR	Furius Purpurio	
CRS29		[illegible]	Horatius	206-200BC
CRS30		L-ITI	L.Iteius	149BC
CRS31		L-IVLI	L.Julius	141BC
CRS32		C-IVNI-C-F	C.Junius	149BC
CRS33		M-IVNI	M.Junius Silanus	145BC
CRS34	TRIO	CN-LVCR	Cn.Lucretius Trio	136BC
CRS35	LIBO	Q-MARC	Q.Marcius Libo	148BC
CRS36		MAT	Matienus	179-170BC
CRS37	RVF	Q-MINV	Q.Minucius Rufus	122BC
CRS38		LP (or above horse)	L.Plautius Hypsaeus	194-190BC*
CRS39		C-PLVT	C.Plutius	121BC
CRS40		T⊗Q		
CRS41		SX-Q	Sextus Quinctilius	189-180BC
CRS42		C-SCR	C.Scribonius	154BC
CRS43		GR	Gracchus	199-170BC
CRS44		L-SEMP	L.Sempronius Pitio	148BC
CRS45		VAR	A.Terentius Varro	206-200BC
CRS46		C-VAR	C.Varro	209-208BC
CRS49		C-TER-LVC	C. Terentius Lucanus	147BC

The Named Coins of the Roman Republic

GROUP 2: Coins Of the "Biga" type (CRS13-14), a biga being a chariot pulled by two creatures of any sort, though most commonly by horses.

Class One: Obverse, helmeted head (usually ROMA): Biga of horses (driver often Victory).

CRS56: VF £30 - £40

CRS89: VF £30 - £40

Ref	Obverse	Reverse	Moneyer	Date
CRS50		SAFRA	Spurius Afranius	150BC
CRS51		SAR	Atilius Saranus	155BC
CRS52		L-ĀILI	L.Atilius Nomentanus	141BC
CRS53		A/	Aurelius	194-190BC
CRS54	L-COSCO-M-F	L-LIC-CN-DOM	L.Cosconius	(S) 118BC
CRS55	C-MALLE-C-F	L-LIC-CN-DOM	C.Malleolus	(S) 118BC
CRS56	L-POMPONI-CNF	L-LIC-CN-DOM	L.Pomponius	(S) 118BC
CRS57	L-PORCI LICI	L-LIC-CN-DOM	L.Porcius Licinius	(S) 118BC
CRS58		SCA/RI RI L-LIC-CN-DOM	M.Aurelius Scaurus	(S) 118BC
CRS59		Elephants head	L.Caecilius Metellus	128BC
CRS60		M-CALID QME-CNFL or C NFOV M-CA-Q-ME	M.Calidus, Q.Metellus & Cn.Fulvius	117-116BC
CRS61		P-CALP	P.Calpurnius	133BC
CRS62	M-CIPI-M-F	Rudder	M.Cipius	115-114BC
CRS63		C-PVLCHER	C.Claudius Pulcher	110-109BC
CRS64		T-CLOVLI	T.Cloelius	128BC
CRS65		CALD or C-COIL CALD	C.Coilius Caldus	104BC
CRS66		P-SVA	P.Sulla	151BC
CRS67		CN-LENTVL	Cn.Lentulus Clodianus	88BC
CRS68		Man fighting dog CN-DOM	Cn.Domitius Ahenobarbus	128BC
CRS69		L-FLAMINICILO or CHILO	F.Flaminius Chilo	109-108BC
CRS70		PVR	Furius Purpurio	179-170BC
CRS71		SEX-IVI CAISAR	Sextus Julius Caesar	129BC
CRS72		L-IVLI	L.Julius	101BC

(S) = "Serrated edge" (as CRS56 Illustration above)

The Named Coins of the Roman Republic

CRS73		D-SILANVS L-F	D.Silanus	91BC
CRS74		Ā	P.Juventius Thalna	179-170BC
CRS75		C-Ā	C.Thalna	154BC
CRS76	PV head within wreath	RVF M-LVCILI	M.Lucilius Rufus	101BC
CRS77		C-MIAVI	C.Maianius	153BC
CRS78		M-MRC	M.Marcius	134BC
CRS79		M-OPEIMI	M.Opimius	131BC
CRS80		NATĀ or NAT	Pinarius Natta	149BC
CRS81		C-CATO	C.Cato	123BC
CRS82	LAECA	M-PORC	M.Porcius Laeca	125BC
CRS83	FLAC	L-RVTILI	L.Rutilius Flaccus	77BC
CRS84		L-SAVF	L.Saufeius	152BC
CRS85	RVLLI	P-SERVILI-M-F	P.Servilius Rullus	100BC
CRS86		A-SPVRI	A.Spurilius	139BC
CRS87		C-TITINI	C.Titinius	141BC
CRS88		L.-TREBAVI	L.Trebanius	135BC
CRS89		FLAC C-VAL-C-F	C.Valerius Flaccus	140BC

Class Two Obv: Helmeted head (usually Roma). Rev: "Biga" of other creatures.

CRS93: VF £30 - £40

Ref	Obverse	Driver	Animal	Reverse	Moneyer	Date
CRS90	COTA	Hercules	Centaurs	M-AVRELI	M.Aurelius Cotta	139BC
CRS91	NASO	Diana	Stags	L-AXSIVS L-F	L.Axius Naso	71BC
CRS92		Jupiter	Elephants	C-METELLVS	C.Caecilius Metellus	125BC
CRS93	CAESAR	Venus	Cupids	L-IVI L-F	L.Julius Caesar	103BC
CRS94		Juno	Goats	C-REN	C.Renius	138BC
CRS95		Cybele	Lions	M-VOLTEI M-F	M.Volteius	78BC

CRS95: VF £30 - £40

The Named Coins of the Roman Republic

Class Three: Obv: Non-helmeted head. Rev: “Biga” of horses (driver often victory)

CRS111: VF £30 - £40

CRS112: VF £30 - £40

CRS113: VF £400

Ref	Obverse	Reverse	Moneyer	Date
CRS96	Female head C-ANNIVS T-F-T-N-PRO-COS	Q-C-TARQVITI P-F	C.Annius & C.Tarquitius	82-81BC
CRS97	Sol, radiate	M AQIL	Manlius Aquillius	109-108BC
CRS98	Victory (wing at shoulder)	T-CARISI	T. Carisius	46BC
CRS99	Diana with bow and quiver	TI CLAVD -TI-F-AP-N	T.Claudius Nero	79BC
CRS100	Venus MAXSVMVS	C-EGNATIUS-CN-F-CN-N	Cn.Egnatius Maxsumus	75BC
CRS101	Cybele veiled and turreted	C-FABI C-F	C.Fabius Hadrianus	102BC
CRS102	Salus SALVS	D-SILANVS L-F	D.Silanus	91BC
CRS103	Mask of Silenus	D-SILANVS L-F	D.Silanus	91BC
CRS104	Venus L-CENSORIN	P-CREPVS C-LIMETAN	L.Censorinus, P.Crepusius and CLimetanus	82BC
CRS105	Saturn	L-MEMMI GAL	L.Memmius Galeria	106BC
CRS106	Saturn	L-C-MEMIES L-F-GAL	L. and C.Memmius Galeria	87BC
CRS107	Victory	L-MVSSIDIVS LONGVS	L.Mussidius Longus	42BC
CRS108	Tatius SABIN	L-TITVRI	L.Titurius Sabinus	89BC
CRS109	Sol, radiate ACISCVLVS	L-VALERIVS	L.Valerius Acisculus	45BC
CRS110	Tatius SABINVS Ā	IVDEX T-VETTIVS	T.Vettius Sabinus	70BC
CRS111*	Juno Sospita	L-PROCILI-F (S)	L.Procilius	80BC
CRS112	Liberty, diademed MENSOR	L-FARSVLEI	L.Farsuleius Mensor	75BC
CRS113*	Vercingetorix (?)	L-HOSTILIVS SASERNA	L.Hostilius Saserna	48BC

(S) = “Serrated edge”

The Named Coins of the Roman Republic

Class Four: Obv: Non-helmeted head. Rev: Non-horse "biga"

CRS116: VF £30 - £40 *

Ref	Obverse	Driver	Animal	Legend	Moneyer	Date
CRS114	Female head	Diana	Stags	C-ALLI	C.Allius Bala	92BC
CRS115	Female head	Neptune	Hippocamps	Q-CREPEREI ROCVS S	Q.Crepereius Rocus	72BC
CRS116*	Bacchus	Ceres	Serpents	M-VOLTEI -M-F	M.Volteius	78BC

GROUP 3: The three-horse "triga"

Ref	Obverse	Reverse	Moneyer	Date
CRS117	Head of Roma	Victory in triga AP-CL-T-M-Q-VR or T-M-AP-CL-Q- VR	T.Manlius Mancinus, Appius Claudius Pulcher and Q.Urbinus	111-110BC
CRS118	Head of Venus	Victory in triga C-NÆ-BAB	C.Naevius Balbus	79BC

The Named Coins of the Roman Republic

GROUP 4: The "Quadriga" drawn by four animals. (Always horses on Republican coins).
Class One: Obv: Helmeted head (usually Roma).

CRS121: VF £30 - £40

CRS149: VF £30 - £40

Ref	Obverse	Reverse	Moneyer	Date
CRS119	GEM	C.ABVRI	C.Aburius Geminus	134BC
CRS120	GEM	M-ABVRI	M.Aburius Geminus	132BC
CRS121	BA BVS in wreath	M-ACILI	Man.Acilius Balbus	125BC
CRS122	M.ACILIVS M F		M.Acilius	130BC
CRS123	C-ANNIVS.T.F.T.N.PRO.COS	L-FABI-L-F-HISP	C.Annius & L.Fabius Hispaniensis	82-81BC
CRS124	CRAG	L-ATES	L.Antestius Gragulus	136BC
CRS125		L-SATVRN	L.Appuleius Saturninus	104BC
CRS126	RVS	M-AF	M.Aufidius Rusticus	140BC
CRS127	Q-ME		Q.Caecilius Metellus	130BC
CRS128		C-CASSI	C.Cassius	126BC
CRS129		C-CONSIDI	C.Considius Paetus	46BC
CRS130	SISENNA	CN-CORNEL-L-F	Cn.Cornelius Sisenna	118-107BC
CRS131	TRIGE	C- C VR	C.Curiatus Trigeminus	142BC
CRS132	Q-CVRT	M-S I A	Q.Curtius	116-115BC
CRS133		CN-DOMI	Cn.Domitius Ahenobarbus	116-115BC
CRS134	LABEO	Q-FABI	C.Fabius Labeo	124BC
CRS135		C-F-L-R-Q-M	C.Fabius, L.Roscus and Q.Marcius	118-117BC
CRS136		Q-MR-C-F-L-R	C.Fabius, L.Roscus and Q.Marcius	118-117BC
CRS137		MAV-C-F	M.Fannius	123BC
CRS138		C-FVNDAN	C.Fundanus	101BC
CRS139	(Head within wreath)	CN-GEL	Cn.Gellius	138BC
CRS140		P-ME-AT	P.Maenius Antiaticus	132BC
CRS141	L-MANLI PRO-Q	L-SVLLA IM	L.Manlus Torquatus	82BC
CRS142		L-MINVCI	L.Minucius	113BC
CRS143		L-OPEIMI	L.Opimius	131BC
CRS144		M-CARBO	M.Carbo	122BC
CRS145		CARB	Cn.Carbo	121BC
CRS146	LAECA	M-PORC	M.Porcius Laeca	125BC
CRS147		L-POST-AB	L.Postumius Albinus	131BC
CRS148	AR G PVB	L-SENTI-C-F	L.Sentius	101BC
CRS149		M-TVLLI	M.Tullius	120BC
CRS150	M-VARG		M.Vargunteius	130BC

The Named Coins of the Roman Republic

Class Two: Obv: Non-helmeted head (or other type). Rev: “Quadriga” of horses.

CRS151 VF £30 - £40

Ref	Obverse	Reverse	Moneyer	Date
CRS151	Jupiter	Q-ATO-BAB PR	Q.Antonius Balbus	83-82BC
CRS152	Victory	T-CARISI	T.Carisius	46BC
CRS153	Venus: PAETI	C-CONSIDI	C.Considius Paetus	46BC
CRS154	Jupiter	L-SCIP-ASIAG	L.Scipio Asiagenus	106BC
CRS155	Vejovis (young male head)	GAR-OGV-VER or OGV-GAR-VER	Gargilius, Ogulnius and Vergilius	86BC
CRS156	Genius (laureate & winged)	IVLI-BVRSIO	L.Julius Bursio	85BC
CRS157	Vejovis (holding thunderbolt)	C-LICINIVS L-F MACER	C.Licinius Macer	84BC
CRS158	Neptune: P-YPSAE	C-YPSAE-COS PRIV CEPIT	P.Plautius Hypsaeus	58BC
CRS159	Female bust: P-YPSAE	C-YPSAE-COS PRIV CEPIT	P.Plautius Hypsaeus	58BC
CRS160	Apollo: PANSA	C-VIBIVS C-F	C.Vibius Pansa	90BC
CRS161*	Jupiter, Juno (illustrated) or Minerva (helmeted) DOS	L-RVBRI	L.Rubrius Dossenus	87BC
CRS162*	Illustrated below		M.Aemilius Scaurus and P.Plautius Hypsaeus	58BC

CRS161: VF £30 - £40 *

CRS162: VF £80 *

The Named Coins of the Roman Republic

GROUP 5: Coins (type with notable Obverse). **Class One:** With Head of Roma as CRS9.

CRS163: T.Didius 113 - 112BC **VF £70 ***

CRS164: M.Caecilius Metellus 127BC **VF £50** *

CRS165: T.Minucius Augurinus 134BC **VF £50 ***

CRS166: T.Minucius Augurinus 135BC **VF £50 ***

CRS167: M.Sergius Silus 116 - 115BC **VF £50** *

CRS168: C.Servilius 136BC **VF £55 ***

CRS169: G.Servilius Vatia 127BC **VF £60**

CRS170: M.Servilius 100BC **VF £55**

CRS171: S.Pompeius Fostlus 137BC **VF £55 ***

CRS172: C.Poblicius 80BC **VF £55** *

Similar Helmeted Heads

CRS173: Mn.Aquillius 71BC **VF £55 ***

CRS174: T.Carisius 46BC **VF £50 ***

CRS175: Cn.Blasio 112 - 111BC **VF £55 ***

CRS176: Q.Lutatius Cerco 109 - 108BC **VF £55 ***

CRS177: Albinus Bruti.f. 48BC **VF £55 ***

CRS178: L.Rustius 76BC **VF £55 ***

The Named Coins of the Roman Republic

CRS179: P.Satrienus 77BC **VF £55 ***

CRS180: L.Torquatus 113 - 112BC **VF £50 ***

CRS181: The Marsic Federation 90 - 89BC (Oscan legends) **VF £300 ***

Class Two: With Two Faces

CRS182: M.Furius Philus 119BC **VF £55 ***

CRS183: C.Fonteius 114-113BC **VF £55 ***

CRS184: C.Sulpicius Galba 106BC **VF £60 ***

CRS185: C.Censorinus 88BC **VF £55 ***

CRS186: M.Junius Brutus 54BC **VF £150 ***

CRS187: C.Coelius Caldus 51BC **VF £200 ***

CRS188: M.Plaetorius Cestianus 67BC **VF £200 ***

Class Three: Front Facing heads

CRS189: L.Plautius Plancus 47BC **VF £80 ***

CRS190: L.Cornelius Lentulus & C.Claudius Marcellus 49BC **VF £55 ***

The Named Coins of the Roman Republic

Class Four: Wearing various crowns, caps, or animal skins.

CRS191: A.Plautius 55BC
VF £55 *

CRS192: L.Plaetorius
Cestianus 67BC **VF £55 ***

CRS193: P.Furius Crassipes
84BC **VF £55 ***

CRS194: L.Philippus
113 - 112BC **VF £60 ***

CRS195: L.Lucretius Trio
76BC **VF £70 ***

CRS196: C.Mamilius
Limetanus 82BC **VF £160 ***

CRS197: Cn.Plancius 55BC
VF £55 *

CRS198: L.Papius 79BC
VF £60 *

CRS199: L.Roscius Fabatus
64BC **VF £60 ***

CRS200: L.Thorius Balbus
105BC **VF £55 ***

CRS201: M.Volteius 78BC **VF £55 ***

GROUP 6: Other denarii, distinguished by *Reverse* types.
Class One a: Two or more human characters or trophies.

CRS202: M.Junius Brutus
54BC **VF £150 ***

CRS203: L.Titurius Sabinus
89BC **VF £60 ***

CRS204: (Rape of Sabine
Women) Obv: as CRS203
89BC **VF £70 ***

The Named Coins of the Roman Republic

CRS205: L.Aemilius Lepidus Paullus 62BC **VF £60 ***

CRS206: L.Caesius 112 - 111BC **VF £55 ***

CRS207: L.Memmius 109 - 108BC **VF £60 ***

CRS208: A.Albinus 96BC **VF £50 ***

CRS209: C.Servilius 57BC **VF £50 ***

CRS210:L.Calpurnius Piso Caesonius & Q.Servilius Caepio 100BC **VF £60 ***

CRS211: L.Caecilius Metellus 96BC **VF £60 ***

CRS212: M.Herennius 108 - 107BC **VF £60 ***

CRS213: Faustus Cornelius Sulla 56BC **VF £70 ***

CRS214: C.Coelius Caldus 51BC **VF £70 ***

Class One b: Two or more animals

CRS215: T.Quinctius 112 - 111BC **VF £55 ***

CRS216: C.Marius Capito 81BC **VF £55 ***

The Named Coins of the Roman Republic

CRS217: L.Cassius Caecianus 102BC
VF £55 *

CRS218: C.Hosidius Geta 68BC
VF £70 *

Class Two: Animal with human

CRS219: Man.Aemilius Lepidus 114-113BC **VF £60 ***

CRS220: P.Crepusius 82BC
VF £55 *

CRS221: L.Marcius Philippus 56BC **VF £60 ***

CRS222: L.Calpurnius Pise Frugi 90BC
Almost identical coin issued 67BC by C.Piso reading C.PISO L.F.FRVG **VF £55 each ***

CRS223: L.Valerius Acisculus 45BC
VF £55 *

CRS224: A.Postumius Albinus 81BC **VF £55 ***

CRS225: Man Fonteius 85BC **VF £55 ***

CRS226: L.Hostilius Saserna 48BC **VF £55 ***

CRS227: L.Lucretius Trio 76BC **VF £60 ***

CRS228: Man.Cordius Rufus 46BC **VF £60 ***

CRS229: A.Postumius Albinus 81BC **VF £55 ***

The Named Coins of the Roman Republic

Class Three a: Single Animal

CRS230: Q.Caecilius Metellus Pius 81BC
VF £60 *

CRS231: Q.Caecilius Metellus Pius Scipio 47 - 46BC **VF £75 ***

CRS232: C.Censorinus 88BC **VF £55 ***

CRS233: C.Postumius 74BC
VF £55 *

CRS234: T.Carisius 46BC
VF £75 *

CRS235: Q.Titius 90BC
VF £55 *

CRS236: Q.Titius 90BC
VF £55 *

CRS237: Q Cassius Longinus 55BC **VF £55 ***

CRS238: L.Aurelius Cotta 105BC **VF £55 ***

CRS239: C.Valerius Flaccus 82BC **VF £55 ***

The Named Coins of the Roman Republic

Class Three b: Single Human

CRS240: L.Hostilius Saserna 48BC **VF £55 ***

CRS241: M.Cato 89BC – with M.Cato.Pro.PR on Obv. 47 - 46BC **VF £55 ***

CRS242: L.Valerius Flaccus 108 - 107BC **VF £55 ***

CRS243: P.Clodius Turrinus 42BC **VF £60 ***

CRS244: L.Censorinus 82BC **VF £60 ***

CRS245: L.Procilius 80BC **VF £60 ***

CRS246: Man.Acilius Glabrio 49BC **VF £60 ***

CRS247: L.Cassius Longinus 63BC **VF £70 ***

CRS248: C.Vibius Pansa 48BC **VF £60 ***

Class Four: Inanimate objects

CRS249: M.Volteius 78BC **VF £70 ***

CRS250: Petillius Capitolinus 43BC **VF £70 ***

CRS251: Q.Cassius Longinus 55BC **VF £70 ***

CRS252: C.Considius Nonianus 57BC **VF £120 ***

CRS253: Lollius Palicanus 45BC **VF £105 ***

CRS254: M.Plaetorius Cestianus 67BC **VF £250 ***

The Named Coins of the Roman Republic

CRS255: L.Scribonius Libo 62BC **VF £50 ***

CRS256: L.Aemilius Paullus & L.Scribonius Libo 62BC **VF £50**

CRS257: L.Furius Brocchus 63BC **VF £55 ***

CRS258: C.Considius Paetus 46BC **VF £55 ***

CRS259: Q.Pomponius Rufus 54BC **VF £60 ***

CRS260: Q.Sicinius 49BC **VF £60 ***

CRS261: M.Plaetorius Cestianus 67BC **VF £55 ***

CRS262: Albinus Bruti F 48BC **VF £55 ***

CRS263: L.Mussidius Longus 42BC **VF £55 ***

CRS264: C.Norbanus 83BC **VF £60 ***

CRS265: L.Torquatus 65BC **VF £80 ***

CRS266: L.Sulla 81BC **VF £85 ***

CRS267: T.Carisius 46BC **VF £80 ***

CRS268: Cn.Lentulus 76 - 75BC **VF £55 ***

CRS269: P.Galba 69BC **VF £60 ***

CRS270: Q.Caecilius Metellus 81BC **VF £55 ***

CRS271: Q.Sicinius and C.Coponius 49BC **VF £55 ***

CRS272: Albinus Bruti F 48BC **VF £70**

The Named Coins of the Roman Republic

GROUP 7: The minor denominations. With exceptions the Quinarii (Half-denarii) and particularly the Sestertii (Quarter-denarii) of the Republic are not very common.

Class One: The Quinarii (usually about 12 – 15mm in diameter)

CRS273: Unnamed of 81BC
VF £30 *

CRS274: C.Egnatuleius 97BC **VF £30 ***

CRS275: T.Cloelius 98BC
VF £30 *

CRS276: C.Fundanius 101BC **VF £30**

CRS277: Cn Lentulus Clodianus 88BC **VF £30**

CRS278: P.Sabinus 99BC
VF £30

CRS279: L.Calpurnius Piso Frugi 90BC **VF £30 ***

CRS280: L.Papius Celsus 45BC **VF £50 ***

CRS281: L.Rubrius Dossenus 87BC **VF £30 ***

CRS282: Q.Titius 90BC **VF £35 ***

CRS283: M.Cato 89BC. If 'M.Cato PRO.PR', then 47 - 46BC **VF £30 each ***

Class Two: The Sestertii (usually about 9 – 11mm in diameter)

CRS284: Man.Cordius Rufus 46BC **VF £60 ***

CRS285: L.Calpurnius Piso Frugi 90BC
VF £60 *

The Imperatorial Period

This is still within the period of the Republic; but these coins were minted in the names of the great men of the Civil War period, which led to the establishment of the Empire. In fact one of these men, Octavian, became the first Emperor, taking the name "Augustus". From here on all coins are Denarii, unless otherwise stated, until **CRS627**.

POMPEY THE GREAT

Born 106BC, killed 48BC

CRS286: Minted 49BC
VF £330 *

CRS287: Minted 49BC
VF £300 *

CRS288: Minted by his son, Cnaeus Pompey 46 - 45BC
VF £150 *

SEXTUS POMPEY

Younger son of Pompey the Great, killed 35BC

CRS289: Minted 42 - 40BC
VF £500 *

CRS290: Minted 42 - 40BC
VF £250 *

CRS291: Minted 42 - 40BC
VF £250 *

JULIUS CAESAR

Assassinated on the Ides of March 44BC

CRS292: 49 - 48BC
VF £150 *

CRS293: 47 - 46BC
VF £150 *

CRS294: 46BC **VF £100 ***

CRS295: 46 - 45BC
VF £150 *

CRS296: 44BC **VF £800 ***

CRS297: 44BC **VF £600 ***

The Imperatorial Period

JULIUS CAESAR (continued)

Commemorative

CRS298: With M.Antony
43BC **VF £600**

CRS299: With Augustus
17BC **VF £500** *

CRS300: Minted 17BC
VF £350 *

BRUTUS

An assassin of Julius Caesar. He had earlier minted **CRS186** and **CRS202** as a mint official! Committed suicide 42BC. His "Imperatorial" coins were all minted 43-42BC

CRS301: VF £300 *

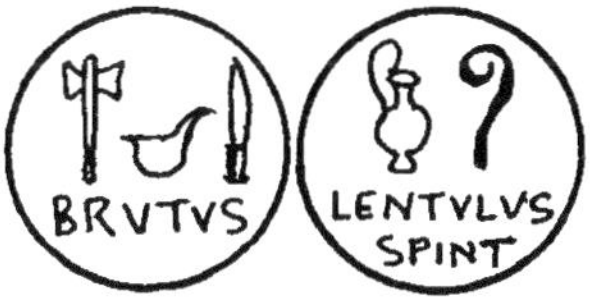

CRS302: VF £300 *

CRS303: VF £300 *

CRS304: VF
Very highly priced *

CRS305: Quinarius
VF £250 *

CRS306: Quinarius
VF £180 *

CASSIUS

Another conspirator in the assassination of Julius Caesar, died 42BC at Philippi

CRS307: Minted 42BC **VF £200** *

The Imperatorial Period

LEPIDUS

A colleague of Antony and Octavian, minted coins 43 - 42BC in conjunction with M. Antony

CRS308: Quinarius **VF £125 ***

MARK ANTONY

Lost Battle of Actium to Octavian in 31BC, killed himself 30BC

CRS309: 42BC
VF £250 *

CRS310: 38 - 37BC
VF £150 *

CRS311: 33BC
VF £250

CRS312: 32 - 31BC **VF £100 ***

CRS313: Quinarius **VF £110** 43BC

MARK ANTONY AND FULVIA

Wife of Mark Antony, married 44BC, died 40BC
Both Quinarii. The features of “Victory” are those of Fulvia

CRS314: 43BC **VF £140 ***

CRS315: 43BC **VF £140 ***

The Imperatorial Period

MARK ANTONY AND OCTAVIA

Married Mark Antony in 40BC, repudiated 32BC

CRS316: Cistophorus of 3 denarii - minted at Ephesus 39 – 38 BC **VF £350 ***

MARK ANTONY AND CLEOPATRA

CRS317: 32-31BC **VF £1,400**

MARK ANTONY AND HIS BROTHER LUCIUS

CRS318: Minted 41BC **VF £600**

MARK ANTONY AND OCTAVIAN

Octavian was soon to be known as "Augustus"

CRS319: 40 - 39BC
VF £300

CRS320: 39BC **VF £220 ***

CRS321: 40 - 39BC
Quinarius
VF £ ?? *

The Imperatorial Period

AUGUSTUS

As Octavian, sharing power, before the Battle of Actium 31BC

CRS322: 42BC **VF £200 ***

CRS323: 41BC **VF £200**

CRS324: 40BC **VF £160 ***

CRS325: 36BC **VF £180 ***

CRS326: 36BC **VF £180**

The Battle of Actium

The battle of Actium was a naval battle in which Octavian (later Augustus) defeated the larger combined fleets of Mark Antony and Cleopatra on the 2nd September 31BC off the coast of Western Greece.

Antony was in Greece with a powerful infantry force and had engaged in indecisive battles with Octavian on land. During this time Octavian's competent naval commander Marcus Agrippa had managed to sever Antony's sea supply route. Mark Antony and Cloepatra tried to negotiate peace terms but were unsuccessful. They then fled to Alexandria in Egypt but Octavian followed them and they surrendered without a fight the following year. Mark Antony committed suicide.

The mighty Roman Empire was born. Octavian was now in complete control. As Emperor he was renamed "Augustus" and became the first of many powerful men to govern and conquer what was at the time, most of the known civilised world.

The Roman Empire

(Octavian as) AUGUSTUS - 31BC - 14AD

CRS327: VF £150 *

CRS328: VF £200 *

CRS329: VF £180 *

CRS330: VF £140

CRS331: VF £170

CRS332: VF £170 *
Obv: as **CRS331**

CRS333: VF £400 *

CRS334: VF £150 *

CRS335: VF £150 *
Obv: as **CRS334**

CRS336: VF £150 *

CRS337: VF £175
Obv: as **CRS336**

CRS338: VF £175 *

CRS339: VF £250 *
Rev: Comet

CRS340: VF £150 *

CRS341: VF £140 *
Obv: as **CRS340**

CRS342: VF £120 *
Main type 2BC – 14AD

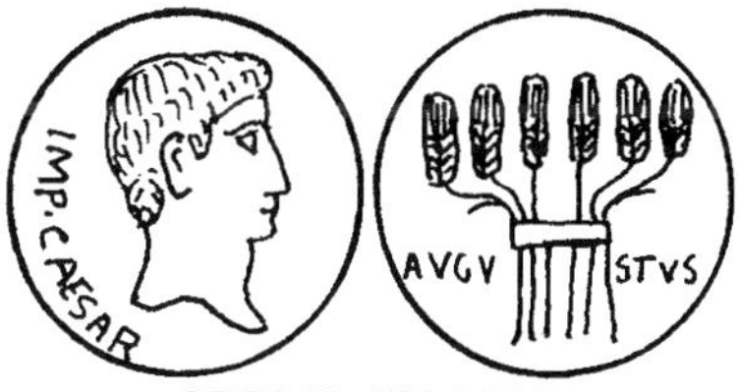

CRS343: VF £300
Cistophorus of three denarii

CRS344: VF £325 *
Obv: as **CRS343**

The Roman Empire

AUGUSTUS - 31BC - 14AD (Continued)

CRS345: VF £80 Quinarius *

CRS346: VF £80 Quinarius *

CRS347: VF £100 *

CRS348: VF £100
Obv: as **CRS347**

CRS347 and **CRS348** are Commemorative Antoniniani (Double-denarii) minted by Trajan Decius 249-251AD

TIBERIUS - 14 - 37AD

CRS349: VF £150 *

CRS349 is the "Tribute Penny" referred to in the New Testament.

CRS350: VF £200 *

CALIGULA - 37 - 41AD

CRS351: VF £700 *

CRS352: VF £600
With Augustus

CRS353: VF £650
With father, Germanicus

CRS354: VF £750
With mother, Agrippina Senior

The Roman Empire

CLAUDIUS I - 41 - 54 AD

CRS355: VF £500 *

CRS356: VF £500 *

CRS357: VF £600 *

CRS358: VF £600 *

CRS359: VF £600 *
Cistophorus of three denarii minted at Ephesus.

CRS360: VF £600 *
Didrachm minted in Cappadocia.

CRS361: VF £700 *
Commemorative, struck under Nero

NERO - 54 - 68 AD

As Caesar under Claudius, 50 – 54 AD

CRS362: VF £350 *

CRS363: VF £300 *

The Roman Empire

NERO - 54 - 68 AD

As Emperor

CRS364: VF £300 *

CRS365: VF £300 *

CRS366: VF £250

CRS367: VF £200

CRS368: VF £200

CRS369: VF £250

CRS370: VF £250

Relations (Augustus to Nero)

CRS371: VF £800 *

Caius Caesar, adopted by Augustus, died 4 AD

CRS372: VF £600

CRS373: VF £600

Nero Claudius Drusus, brother of Tiberius, father of Claudius, died 9 BC

CRS374: VF £1000 *

Antonia, wife of Nero Claudius Drusius, mother of Claudius, died 37AD.

CRS375: VF £750

Agrippina Junior & Claudius

CRS376: VF £750

Agrippina Junior & Nero

Agrippina Junior was the wife of Claudius and mother of Nero. She died 59 AD. CRS375 and CRS376 were minted during the reign of Claudius.

The Roman Empire

CLODIUS MACER - 68 AD

Rebelled against Nero April 68AD, died October 68 AD

CRS377: VF Very rare and highly priced

NOTE: From this reign onwards, obverse legends become greatly varied, as do reverse types! However, for the collector it is normally far more important to work out which Emperor a coin should be attributed to, rather that what the reverse type is. Therefore the different obverses are listed first, followed by just a sample few reverses. What the reverse happens to be will not usually affect the price except in cases of special interest.

GALBA - 68 - 69 AD

From 9th June 68 AD – 15th January 69 AD

Obverse A

Obverse B

Obverse C

Obverse D

Obverse E

CRS378: VF £300
With Obverse A

CRS379: VF £300 *
With Obverse C

CRS380: VF £252
Quinarius

OTHO - 69 AD

From 15th January 69 AD – 17th April 69 AD

Obverse A

Obverse B

CRS381: VF £500

CRS382: VF £500

CRS383: VF £500

CRS384: VF £500

The Roman Empire

VITELLIUS - 69 AD

Proclaimed in Germany, 2nd January 69 AD – 20th December 69 AD

Obverse A

Obverse B

Obverse C

Obverse D

CRS385: VF £300

CRS386: VF £300

CRS387: VF £300 *

CRS388: VF £300

CRS389: VF £300

CRS390: VF £900+
Vitellius' Children

Anonymous Coins of the Civil War Period 68 – 69 AD

At first sight some of these 68 - 69AD types (there are many types; but all are fairly uncommon) may be confused with the Republican series. These later coins do not state the name of any mint official.

CRS391: VF £350

CRS392: VF £400

CRS393: VF £450

CRS394: VF £450 *

CRS395: VF £450

The Roman Empire

VESPASIAN - 69 - 79 AD

Proclaimed in Alexandria, Egypt, 1st July 69 AD – 24th June 79 AD

Obverse A

Obverse B

Obverse C

Obverse D

Obverse E

Obverse F

Obverse G

CRS396: VF £45 *

CRS397: VF £45

CRS398: VF £45

CRS399: VF £45

CRS400: VF £150 *
With Obverse D

CRS401: VF £300
His sons Titus & Domitian.

Obverse H
Commemorative

Obverse I
Commemorative

CRS402: VF £50

CRS403: VF £100

With Obv H. Struck during the reign of Titus.

CRS404: Antoninianus
VF £100 *
With Obv I. 249 – 251 AD

The Roman Empire

TITUS - 79 - 81 AD

As Caesar under Vespasian 69 – 79 AD

Obverse A

Obverse B

Obverse C

CRS405: VF £80 *

CRS406: VF £80

CRS407: VF £125
Quinarius

TITUS - 79 - 81 AD

As Emperor

Obverse D

Obverse E

CRS408: VF £80

CRS409: VF £80

CRS410: VF £80 *

CRS411: VF £80

CRS412: VF £120
Commemorative Antoninianus 249 – 251 AD

The Roman Empire

JULIA TITI

Daughter of Titus

CRS413: VF £500 *

DOMITIAN - 91 - 96 AD

As Caesar under Vcspasian and Titus, 69 – 81 AD

Obverse A

Obverse B

Obverse C

CRS414: VF £60

CRS415: VF £60 *

CRS416: VF £60 *

CRS417: VF £60 *

DOMITIAN - 91 - 96 AD As Emperor

Obverse D

Obverse E

Obverse F

Obverse G

CRS418: VF £40 *

CRS419: VF £40 *

CRS420: VF £80

CRS421: VF £100

CRS422: Quinarius **VF £125**

DOMITIA

Wife of Domitian from 82 AD

CRS423: VF £1000 *

CRS424: VF £1200 *

NERVA - 96 - 98 AD

Obverse A

Obverse B

CRS425: VF £100

CRS426: VF £100

CRS427: VF £100

CRS428: VF £100 *

CRS429: Quinarius
VF £300

CRS430: VF £100
Commemorative Antoninianus
Minted 249 – 251 AD

TRAJAN - 98 - 117 AD

Obverse A

Obverse B

Obverse C

CRS431: VF £40 *

CRS432: VF £40 *

CRS433: VF £40 *

CRS434: VF £70

CRS435: VF £65 *

CRS436: VF £60 *

CRS437: Quinarius
VF £120

The Roman Empire

TRAJAN - 98 - 117 AD (continued)

CRS438: Cistophorus (3 Denarii)
VF £200

CRS439: VF £100
Commemorative Antoninianus of 249 – 251 AD. Rev: Altar or Eagle as CRS347 and CRS348. (CONSECRATIO)

CRS440: VF £600
During his reign Trajan reissued a large number of Republican and earlier Imperial types, adding his own name and titles on the reverse: but all these "restored" coins are rare.

PLOTINA

Wife of Trajan, died 129AD

CRS441: VF £1000 *

MARCIANA

Sister of Trajan, died 114 AD

CRS442: VF £1000

MATIDIA

Niece of Trajan, died 119 AD

CRS443: VF £1000 *

CRS444: VF £1000

HADRIAN - 117 - 138 AD

Obverse A

Obverse B

Obverse C

Obverse D

Obverse E

CRS445: VF £45 *

CRS446: VF £60 *

CRS447: VF £55

CRS448: VF £50

CRS449: VF £40

CRS450: VF £40

CRS451: VF £45

CRS452: Quniarius
VF £100

CRS453: VF £250
Cistophorus of 3 denarii

CRS454: VF £100
Minted in reign of
Antoninus Pius

CRS455:
Antoninianus
VF £100
Reverse:
"CONSECRATIO"
Altar or Eagle.
249 – 241 AD

The Roman Empire

SABINA

Wife of Hadrian, died 137 AD

Obverse A

Obverse B

Obverse C

CRS456: VF £60

CRS457: VF £60

CRS458: VF £100
Commemorative

AELIUS, Caesar - 136 - 138 AD

Obverse A

Obverse B

CRS459: VF £150

CRS460: VF £150

ANTONINUS PIUS - 138 - 161 AD

As Caesar under Hadrian, 25th February 138 AD – 10th July 138 AD

Obverse A

CRS461: VF £50

The Roman Empire

ANTONINUS PIUS - 138 - 161 AD, As Emperor

Obverse B

Obverse C

Obverse D

Obverse E

Obverse F

Obverse G

CRS462: VF £30 *

CRS463: VF £30

CRS464: VF £30

CRS465: VF £30

CRS466: VF £35

CRS467: VF £30 *

CRS468: VF £60
With Marcus Aurelius

ANTONINUS PIUS - 138 - 161 AD, Commemorative

Obverse H

CRS469: VF £35

CRS470: VF £35 *

CRS471: VF £45 *

CRS472: VF £45

Left:
"CONSECRATIO"
Antoninianus.
249 – 251 AD
Rev: Altar or Eagle
As CRS347 or CRS348

FAUSTINA SENIOR

Wife of Antoninus Pius, died 141 AD

During her Lifetime

Obverse A

Obverse B

CRS473: VF £35

After her Death

Obverse C

Obverse D

Obverse E

Obverse F

CRS474: VF £35

CRS475: VF £35

CRS476: VF £45

MARCUS AURELIUS - 161 - 180 AD

As Caesar under Antoninus Pius, 139 – 161 AD

Obverse A

Obverse B

Obverse C

CRS477: VF £35 *

CRS478: VF £35

The Roman Empire

MARCUS AURELIUS - 161 - 180 AD

As Emperor

Obverse D

Obverse E

Obverse F

Obverse G

Obverse H

Obverse I

Obverse J

CRS479: VF £30 *

CRS480: VF £35 *

CRS481: VF £30

CRS482: VF £30 *

CRS483: VF £30

CRS484: Quinarius **VF £200**

CRS485: VF £45
Commemorative, minted by Commodus

FAUSTINA JUNIOR

Married Marcus Aurelius 145 AD, died 175 AD

Obverse A

CRS486: VF £40

CRS487: VF £40 *

Obverse B

CRS488: VF £35

CRS489: VF £35

CRS490: VF £35 *

CRS491: VF £35 *

CRS492: VF £40 *

The Roman Empire

FAUSTINA JUNIOR, Commemorative

Obverse C

Obverse D

CRS493: VF £40

CRS494: VF £40

CRS495: VF £40 *

LUCIUS VERUS - 161 - 169 AD

Co-Emperor with Marcus Aurelius

Obverse A

Obverse B

Obverse C

Obverse D

CRS496: VF £40

CRS497: VF £40

CRS498: VF £45 *

Commemorative

Obverse E

CRS499: VF £50

CRS500: VF £50

The Roman Empire

LUCILLA

Daughter of Marcus Aurelius, married Verus in 164 AD

Obverse A

Obverse B

CRS501: VF £45

CRS502: VF £45

CRS503: VF £50

COMMODUS - 177 - 192 AD

As Caesar under Marcus Aurelius, 175 – 177 AD

Obverse A

CRS504: VF £40

CRS505: VF £40

As Emperor

Obverse B

Obverse C

Obverse D

Obverse E

Obverse F

Obverse G

Obverse H

The Roman Empire

COMMODUS - 177 - 192 AD (continued)

CRS506:
VF £40 *

CRS507:
VF £40 *

CRS508:
VF £70 *

CRS509:
VF £70 *

CRS510:
VF £80 *
With Obv H

CRISPINA

Married Commodus 177 AD, put to death 183 AD

Obverse A

Obverse B

CRS511:
VF £50

CRS512:
VF £60

CRS513:
VF £50

PERTINAX - 1st January 193 – 28th March 193 AD

Obverse A

CRS514:
VF £600

CRS515:
VF £600

CRS516: VF £750
Commemorative, minted under Septimius Severus

DIDIUS JULIANUS - 28th March 193 – 2nd June 193

CRS517: VF £750

CRS518: VF £1000
His Wife MANLIA SCANTILLA

CRS519: VF £1000+
His daughter DIDIA CLARA

The Roman Empire

PESCENNIUS NIGER - 193 - 194 AD

Proclaimed April 193 AD, Killed Autumn 194 AD

Obverse A

Obverse B

CRS520: VF £750

CRS521: VF £750

CLODIUS ALBINUS - 195 - 197 AD

Proclaimed Emperor in Gaul autumn 195 AD, died 19th February 197 AD

As Caesar under Septimius Severus 193 – 195 AD

Obverse A

Obverse B

CRS522: VF £120

CRS523: VF £120

As Emperor 195 – 197 AD

Obverse C

Obverse D

Obverse E

CRS524: VF £150 *

CRS525: VF £150

SEPTIMIUS SEVERUS - 193 - 211 AD

Obverse A

Obverse B

Obverse C

Obverse D

Obverse E

Obverse F

Obverse G

CRS526: VF £25 *

CRS27: VF £25

CRS528: VF £25 *

The Roman Empire

SEPTIMIUS SEVERUS - 193 - 211 AD (continued)

CRS529: VF £90

CRS530: VF £200

CRS531: VF £30

CRS532: VF £30 *

CRS532: VF £50

CRS534: Quinarius **VF £200**

CRS535: Cistophorus of three denarii **VF £200**

Commemorative minted by Caracalla and Geta

Obverse H

CRS536: VF £30

CRS537: VF £30 *

SEVERUS WITH JULIA DOMNA

CRS538: VF £150

SEVERUS WITH CARACALLA

CRS539: VF £150

CARACALLA - 198 - 217 AD

Note: During this reign, at the end of 214 AD, the double-denarius, known as the Antoninianus, named after himself (as "ANTONINUS PIUS" rather than "CARACALLA") was introduced.

As Caesar 196 – 198 AD

Obverse A

Obverse B

CRS540: VF £35

CRS541: VF £35

CRS542: VF £35

As Emperor

At first with Septimius Severus, then with Geta and then by himself from 212 AD

Obverse C

Obverse D

Obverse E

Obverse F

Obverse G

Obverse H

CRS543: VF £25

CRS544: VF £25 *

CRS545: VF £25 *

CRS546: VF £25 *

CRS547: VF £50 *

CRS548: VF £200 *

CRS549: Quinarius **VF £250**

CRS550: Cistophorus of 3 denarii **VF £200**

The Roman Empire

CARACALLA - 198 - 217 AD (continued)

Obverse I

CRS551: VF £65

CRS552: VF £65 *

The new ANTONINIANUS, distinguished on males by the radiate crown

CRS553: VF £30

Commemorative

GETA - 209 - 212 AD

As Caesar 198 - 209 AD

Obverse A

Obverse B

Obverse C

Obverse D

CRS554: VF £35 *

CRS555: VF £35

CRS556: VF £125

As Emperor with Septimius Severus, then with Caracalla

Obverse E

Obverse F

Obverse G

CRS557: VF £40 *

CRS558: VF £40 *

CRS559: VF £45 *

MACRINUS - April 217 - June 218 AD

Obverse A

Obverse B

CRS560: VF £100 *

CRS561: VF £100 *

Obverse C
Antoninianus

CRS562: VF £300
Antoninianus

DIADUMENIAN - 218 AD

Son of Macrinus, proclaimed Caesar April 217 AD, proclaimed Co-emperor with Macrinus just before his father's death June 218 AD.

Obverse A

CRS563: VF £170 *

CRS564: VF £170

There is an "excessively rare, if not unique" denarius of Diadumenian as Emperor.

ELAGABALUS - Proclaimed in Syria - 16th May 218 - 222 AD

Note: Heads and legends are interchangeable, i.e. legend F can be used on the denarius, and legends A - E on the Antoninianus.

Obverse A

Obverse B

Obverse C

Obverse D

Obverse E

Obv: E (with the horn), is used with reverses showing Elagabalus sacrificing, e.g. **CRS570 and CRS571**

The Roman Empire

ELAGABALUS - 16th May 218 - 222 AD (continued)

CRS565: VF £25

CRS566: VF £25

CRS267: VF £25

CRS568: VF £25 *

CRS569: VF £200 *

CRS570: VF £25 *

CRS571: VF £25 *

The Antoniniani

Obverse F

CRS572: VF £60

CRS573: VF £60

SEVERUS ALEXANDER - 222 - 235 AD

As Caesar under Elagabalus 221 - 222 AD

Obverse A

CRS574: VF £25

CRS575: VF £25 *

As Emperor

The Antoninianus was not minted during this reign, and was not reintroduced until 238 AD (under Balbinus & Pupienus).

Obverse B

Obverse C

Obverse D

Obverse E

Obverse F

The Roman Empire

SEVERUS ALEXANDER - 222 - 235 AD (continued)

CRS576:
VF £25 *

CRS577:
VF £25

CRS578:
VF £25

CRS579:
VF £25 *

CRS580: Quinarius **VF £400**

Commemorative

Obverse G

CRS581: VF £100 *
Antoninianus of
249 – 251 AD

CRS582: VF £100
Antoninianus of
249 – 251 AD

The Ladies of the Severan Dynasty 193 – 235 AD

For the Antoninianus denominations ladies have a crescent behind the shoulder

JULIA DOMNA

Wife of Septimius Severus, mother of Caracalla and Geta, died 217 AD

Obverse A

Obverse B

Both used during the reign of Septimius Severus

Obverse C

Used during the reign of Caracalla

The Roman Empire – Ladies of the Severan Dynasty

JULIA DOMNA (continued)

CRS583:
VF £25

CRS584:
VF £25

CRS585:
VF £25

CRS586:
VF £25 *

CRS587: VF £300
Caracalla and Geta

CRS588: Quinarius **VF £400**

Obverse D

CRS589: Antoninianus
VF £80 *

CRS590: Antoninianus
VF £75

Commemorative (reign of Elagabalus)

CRS591: VF £500

PLAUTILLIA

Married to Caracalla in 202 AD, banished 205 AD

Obverse A

Obverse B

Obverse C

CRS592:
VF £40

CRS593:
VF £40 *

CRS594:
VF £40

The Roman Empire – Ladies of the Severan Dynasty

JULIA PAULA

First wife of Elagabalus, married 219 AD, divorced 220 AD

Obverse A

CRS595: VF £80

CRS596: VF £80

AQUILIA SEVERA

One of the Vestal Virgins, became Elagabalus' second wife 220 AD

CRS597: VF £100

JULIA MAESA – Died c223 AD

Sister of Julia Domna. Mother of Julia Soaemias and Julia Mamaea. Grandmother of Elagabalus and Severus Alexander. Lifetime coins were minted during the reign of Elagabalus. The commemorative coins were struck during the reign of Severus Alexander

Obverse A

CRS598: VF £35 *

CRS599: VF £35 *

CRS600: VF £35

CRS601: VF £70
Only Antoninianus type

CRS602: VF £300 *
Commemorative

The Roman Empire – Ladies of the Severan Dynasty

JULIA SOAEMIAS

Daughter of Julia Maesa, mother of Elagabalus.
Killed at the same time as Elagabalus in 222AD.

Obverse A

Obverse B

CRS603: VF £50

CRS604: VF £50

CRS605: VF £50

JULIA MAMAEA

Sister of Julia Domna, mother of Severus Alexander, whom she to a great extent controlled.
Assassinated with Severus Alexander 235 AD.

Obverse

CRS606: VF £25

CRS607: VF £25

CRS608: VF £25

SALLUSTIA BARBIA ORBIANA

Married Severus Alexander 225 AD, but Julia Mamaea became jealous, and made Severus Alexander banish her to Africa c227AD.

CRS609: VF £100

The Roman Empire

MAXIMINUS I - 235 - 238 AD

Obverse A

Obverse B

CRS610a: VF £35

CRS610b: VF £35

CRS611: VF £35

CRS612: VF £35 *

PAULINA

Wife of Maximinus – commemorative coins only, possibly died before Maximinus' accession

Obverse A

CRS613: VF £300

CRS614: VF £300 *

MAXIMUS - Caesar 235 - 238 AD

Son of Maximinus I

Obverse A

Obverse B

CRS615: VF £160 *

CRS616: VF £150

GORDIAN I 238 AD

Proclaimed in North Africa - 22nd March 238, died 12th April 238

CRS617: VF £800

GORDIAN II 238 AD

Son of Gordian I Proclaimed in North Africa 22nd March 238, died 12th April 238

CRS618: VF £800 *

These two Emperors use the same Obverse legend. Coins are distinguished by Gordian II having a bald forehead

BALBINUS & PUPIENUS - 238 AD

Joint Reign 22nd April 238 – 29th July 238 AD. Reintroduced the Antoninianus (Double denarius)

BALBINUS

Obverse A

CRS619: VF £250

CRS620: VF £250

Obverse B Antoninianus

CRS621: Antoninianus **VF £250**

PUPIENUS

Obverse A

CRS622: VF £250

CRS623: VF £250

Obverse B Antoninianus

Obverse C Antoninianus

CRS624: Antoninianus **VF £250**

GORDIAN III - 29th July 238 - 244 AD

Nephew of Gordian II. As Caesar under Balbinus and Pupienus from about May 238 AD

Obverse A

CRS625: VF £200

The Roman Empire

GORDIAN III - 29th July 238 - 244 AD, As Emperor

The Denarii

Obverse B

CRS626: VF £40

CRS627: VF £40

The Antoninianus

The Antoninianus now replaces the Denarius as the main silver coin of the Roman monetary system (until **CRS720**). Unless otherwise stated, all coins of this next "Radiate" period are Antoniniani

Obverse C

Obverse D

CRS628: VF £20

CRS629: VF £20

CRS630: VF £20

CRS631: VF £20 *

CRS632: Quinarius **VF £100**

TRANQUILLINA

Married Gordian III in 241 AD

CRS633: VF Very Rare and Expensive

PHILIP I - 244 - 249 AD

Obverse A

Obverse B

Obverse C

CRS634: VF £20

CRS635: VF £20

CRS636: VF £25

CRS637: VF £25 *

CRS638: VF £30

CRS639: VF £30

CRS640: VF £25

CRS641: VF £30

CRS642: VF £30

OTACILIA SEVERA

Wife of Philip I

Obverse A

Obverse B

Obverse C

CRS643: VF £25

CRS644: VF £25

CRS645: VF £25

CRS646: VF £50

Philip II 247 – 249 AD

Philip I and Philip II can be distinguished by the youthfulness of Phillip II (who was only about twelve when he was killed).

As Caesar under his father Philip I

Obverse A

CRS647: VF £25

CRS648: VF £25

PHILIP II - 247 - 249 AD

As Emperor

Obverse B

Obverse C

Obverse D

CRS649: VF £25

CRS650: VF £30 *

CRS651: VF £35

PACATIAN - 248 AD

Rebel in the Danube region for a few weeks, summer of 248 AD

CRS652: VF Very Rare & expensive

JOTAPIAN - 248 AD

Rebel in Syria for a few weeks, summer of 248 AD

CRS653: VF Very Rare & expensive

The Roman Empire

TRAJAN DECIUS - 249 - 251 AD

Obverse A

Obverse B

CRS654: VF £25

CRS655: VF £25

CRS656: VF £25

CRS657: VF £25 *

Obverse C
Quinarius

Obverse D
Quinarius

CRS658: Quinarius
VF £250

HERENNIA ETRUSCILLA

Wife of Trajan Decius

Obverse A

Obverse B

CRS659: VF £25

CRS660: VF £25

CRS661: VF £25

HERENNIUS ETRUSCUS - 251 AD

Elder son of Trajan Decius.

As Caesar, September 250 – May 251 AD

Obverse A

Obverse B

CRS662: VF £50

CRS663: VF £50

CRS664: VF £50

CRS665: VF £50

As Emperor, May 251 – June 251 AD

Obverse A

CRS666: VF £200

HOSTILIAN

Younger son of Trajan Decius.
Died of plague c Nov.251AD

As Caesar, December 250 - c July 251AD

Obverse A

Obverse B

CRS667: VF £70

CRS668: VF £70

CRS669: VF £70

The Roman Empire

HOSTILIAN - As Emperor, with Trebonianus Gallus c July 251.

Obverse C

Obverse D

CRS670: VF £150

CRS671: VF £175

TREBONIANUS GALLUS - 251 - 253 AD

Obverse A

Obverse B

CRS672: VF £25

CRS673: VF £25

CRS674: VF £25

CRS675: VF £30

CRS676: Quinarius **VF £250**

VOLUSIAN - 251 - 253 AD

Caesar under Trebonianus Gallus c July - c November 251 AD
Co-emperor c November 251 AD - Summer 253 AD

As Caesar

Obverse A

CRS677: VF £100

The Roman Empire

VOLUSIAN - 251 - 253 AD, As Emperor

Obverse B

Obverse C

CRS678: VF £30

CRS679: VF £30

CRS680: VF £80

AEMILIAN - 253 AD

Proclaimed Emperor in Moesia summer 253, assassinated Autumn 253 AD

Obverse A

Obverse B

CRS681: VF £150

CRS682: VF £150

CRS683: VF £150

CORNELIA SUPERA

Wife of Aemilian

Obverse A

CRS684: VF Very rare & expensive

VALERIAN I - 253 - 260 AD

c September 253 – c June 260 AD (when captured by the Persians)

Obverse A

Obverse B

Obverse C

Obverse D

The Roman Empire

VALERIAN I - 253 - 260 AD (continued)

CRS685:
VF £20

CRS686:
VF £20

CRS687:
VF £25 *

CRS688:
VF £25 *

CRS689:
VF £25 *

CRS690: VF £25

CRS691: Denarius **VF £150**

CRS692: Quinarius
VF £150

MARINIANA

Wife of Valerian – Commemorative

CRS693: VF £120

VALERIAN II - 256 - 258 AD

Son of Gallienus, grandson of Valerian I, Caesar 256 – 258 AD

Obverse A

Obverse B

Obverse C

Obverse D

Obverse E

The Roman Empire

VALERIAN II - 256 - 258 AD (continued)

CRS694a:
VF £25

CRS694b:
VF £25

CRS695:
VF £25 *

CRS696:
VF £35 *

Commemorative

Obverse F

Obverse G

CRS697:
VF £25 *

CRS698:
VF £25

CRS699:
VF £25

SALONINUS - 258 - 259 AD

Younger brother of Valerian II. Caesar from 258 – 259 AD. Proclaimed Emperor by his troops besieged in Cologne. His reign lasted just a few weeks until Cologne fell to Postumus

As Caesar

Obverse A

Obverse B

Obverse C

CRS700:
VF £35

CRS701:
VF £35

CRS702:
VF £35

CRS703:
VF £35 *

SALONINUS - 258 - 259 AD, As Emperor

CRS704: VF £300

The Antoninianus is at this stage becoming more and more debased, and by around 26OAD it becomes virtually a base metal coin. The Antoniniani of Gallienus, Salonina, Macrianus, Quietus and Postumus are all included in "**Roman Base Metal Coins – A Price Guide**" (ISBN 0948964-46-4); but as some of their coins do still look "silverish" I list them here also. Prices given are for well-silvered specimens.

GALLIENUS - 253 - 268 AD

Obverse A

Obverse B

Obverse C

Obverse D

Obverse E

Obverse F

CRS705: VF £25

CRS706: VF £25

CRS707: VF £30 *

CRS708: VF £35 *

CRS709: VF £90 *

SALONINA

Wife of Gallienus.

Obverse A

Obverse B

CRS710:
VF £25

CRS711:
VF £25

CRS712:
VF £25

CRS713:
VF £30 *

POSTUMUS - 260 - 269 AD

Rebelled against Gallienus, and ruled over Spain, Gaul and Britain.

Obverse

CRS714:
VF £25 *

CRS715:
VF £35

CRS716:
VF £30

CRS717:
VF £35

CRS718:
VF £120 *

MACRIANUS
c September 260 – Spring 261 AD

CRS719: VF £100

QUIETUS
c September 260 – c November 261 AD

CRS720: VF £100

Macrianus and his brother Quietus were proclaimed Emperors by the remnants of Valerian's army after the latter's capture by the Persians.

From this time until the reign of Carausius in Britain there is no Roman silver coinage

CARAUSIUS - 287 - 293 AD

Emperor in Britain. Carausius minted a small number of Denarii of good silver c 287 – 289 AD. These are all very rare and expensive. It is thought that they may have been an "ACCESSION DONATIVE" to the troops

Obverse

CRS721: VF £1500

CRS722: VF £1500 *

CRS723: VF £1500 *

CRS724: VF £1000

DIOCLETIAN - 284 - 305 AD

Diocletian reformed the system by which the Roman Empire was governed. In 293AD he established the "Tetrarchy" (rule of four people); there were to be two senior Emperors, the "Augusti", and two juniors, the "Caesars" - with himself in charge as senior Augustus. With regard to the coinage, all mints, whichever of the four ruled that particular area were to mint coins in the names of all four rulers. Amongst his numismatic reforms Diocletian introduced a new silver coin known as the "Argenteus", valued at five AE folles.

Obverse

CRS725: VF £200 *

CRS726: VF £200 *

CRS727: VF £200 *

CRS728: VF £200

CRS729: VF £200

CRS730: VF £200

CRS731: VF £250 *

MAXIMIANUS HERCULEUS
286 – 305 AD, 306 – 308 AD and 310 AD

Obverse

CRS732:
VF £200

CRS733:
VF £200

CRS734:
VF £200

CRS735:
VF £200

CONSTANTIUS I
Caesar 293 – 305 AD. Augustus 305 – 306 AD

Obverse

CRS736: VF £200

CRS737: VF £200

GALERIUS also known as MAXIMIANUS
Caesar 293 – 305 AD. Augustus 305 – 311 AD

Obverse

CRS738:
VF £200

CRS739:
VF £200

CRS740:
VF £200

CRS741: Half Argenteus
VF £250

LICINIUS I - 308 - 324 AD

CRS742: VF £100 *

Billon; but considered by some authorities to be a base silver Argenteus.

CONSTANTINE I

Caesar 306 – 307 AD. Augustus 307 – 337 AD

CRS743: VF £500

CRS744: VF £300
Half Argenteus

During the 320's Constantine introduced the Siliqua (which during its early life was the same weight as the Argenteus) and also the Miliarense, which weighed 4.5 grammes as opposed to c 3.4 grammes for the Siliqua. The Miliarense was valued one-third more than the Siliqua. From now on until **CRS841**, all coins are Siliquae unless otherwise stated. In some catalogues the pre 355 AD Siliqua is still called "Argenteus".

CRS745: VF £300

CONSTANTINE II

Caesar 317 – 337 AD. Augustus 337 – 340 AD

As Caesar

CRS746: VF £300

CRS747: VF £350

As Augustus

CRS748: VF £300

CRS749: VF £350

The Roman Empire

CONSTANS - 337 - 350 AD

CRS750: VF £150

CRS751: VF £250

CRS752: VF £300

CRS753: Miliarense **VF £600+**

CONSTANTIUS II

Caesar 324 – 337 AD. Augustus 337 – 361 AD

As Caesar

CRS754: VF £200

CRS755: Miliarense **VF £600**

As Augustus

CRS756:
VF £100

CRS757:
VF £250

CRS758:
VF £80 *

CRS759: VF £80

CRS760: VF £80

The Roman Empire

CONSTANTIUS II (continued)

CRS761: Miliarense **VF £600+**

CRS762: Miliarense **VF £600+**

Around 355 AD the weight and size of the Siliqua was reduced by about a third from average 3.4 grammes to average 2.25 grammes. Whilst Siliquae of Constantius II and other rulers before this date are "unreduced", those after 355 AD are "reduced".

CRS763: VF £45

CRS764: "Reduced" Siliqua **VF £50**

CRS765: VF £45

MAGNENTIUS 350 – 353 AD

Usurper in the West

CRS766: "Unreduced" Siliqua **VF £400 ***

DECENTIUS 351 – 353 AD

Son of Magnentius

CRS767: "Unreduced" Siliqua **VF £1500+**

CONSTANTIUS GALLUS 351 – 354 AD

Caesar under Constantus II

CRS768: "Unreduced" Siliqua **VF £400**

CRS769: "Unreduced" Siliqua **VF £400**

The Roman Empire

JULIAN II - 360 - 363 AD

As Caesar, 355 – 360 AD

CRS770: VF £50

CRS771: VF £150

NOTE: All Siliquae from now on are "reduced"

As Augustus, 360 - 363 AD

CRS772: VF £40

CRS773: VF £40

CRS774: VF £45

CRS775: Miliarense **VF £600+**

JOVIAN - 363 - 364 AD

CRS776: VF £80

VALENTINIAN I - 364 - 375 AD

CRS777: VF £50

CRS778: VF £60 *

CRS779: VF £60

CRS780: VF £50

CRS781: VF £50

The Roman Empire

VALENTINIAN I - 364 - 375 AD

CRS782: Miliarense **VF £400+**

CRS783: Miliarense **VF £400+**

VALENS - 364 - 378 AD

CRS784: VF £40

CRS785: VF £45

CRS786: VF £40

CRS787: VF £40
Obv as **CRS786**

CRS788: VF £40
Obv as **CRS786**

CRS789: VF £40
Obv as **CRS786**

CRS790: VF £40
Obv as **CRS786**

CRS791: Miliarense **VF £400+**

CRS792: Miliarense **VF £400+**

CRS793: Miliarense **VF £400+**

PROCOPIUS - 365 - 366 AD

Rebel in Constantinople area

CRS794: VF £600

GRATIAN - 367 - 383 AD

CRS795: VF £60

CRS796: VF £250 *

CRS797: VF £50

CRS798: VF £50 *

CRS799: VF £50

CRS800: VF £50

CRS801: Miliarense **VF £400+**

VALENTINIAN II - 375 - 392 AD

CRS802: VF £60

CRS803: VF £60

CRS804: VF £60

CRS805: VF £60

CRS806: VF £60

CRS807: Half Siliqua **VF £200**

CRS808: Miliarense **VF £400+**

THEODOSIUS I - 379 - 395 AD

CRS809: VF £60

CRS810: VF £60

CRS811: VF £60

CRS812: VF £60

CRS813: VF £60

CRS814: VF £60

CRS815: Miliarense **VF £400+**

MAGNUS MAXIMUS - 383 - 388 AD

Rebel in the West

CRS816: VF £100

CRS817: VF £80

CRS818: VF £100

FLAVIUS VICTOR 387 – 388 AD

Son of Magnus Maximus

CRS819: VF £200

CRS820: VF £400

The Roman Empire

EUGENIUS - 392 - 394 AD

Ruler in the West

CRS821: VF £200

CRS822: VF £200

ARCADIUS - 393 - 408 AD

CRS823: VF £50

CRS824: VF £50

CRS825: VF £60

HONORIUS - 393 - 423 AD

CRS826: VF £50

CRS827: VF £60

CRS828: Half Siliqua **VF £100**

CRS829: Miliarense **VF £500+**

CONSTANTINE III - 407 - 411 AD

Usurper in the West

CRS830: VF £250

The Roman Empire

CONSTANS 408 – 411 AD

Son of Constantine III

CRS831: VF £1500+

MAXIMUS 409 – 411 AD

Usurper in Spain

CRS832: VF £1500+

JOVINUS 411 – 413 AD

Rebel in Gaul

CRS833: VF £300

CRS834: VF £300

GALLA PLACIDIA

Daughter of Theodosius I, mother of Valentinian III, lived 388 – 450 AD

CRS835: Half Siliqua **VF £500** *

THEODOSIUS II - 402 - 450 AD

CRS836: VF £100

CRS837: VF £100

CRS838: VF £100

Note that 'CONS' is the only mintmark for Theodosius II's 'VOT' type, and this distinguishes **CRS837** from **CRS814** (Theodosius I has various mint marks, but NOT 'CONS')

The Roman Empire

THEODOSIUS II - 402 - 450 AD (continued

CRS839: Miliarense **VF £400+**

PULCHERIA

Daughter of Arcadius, elder sister of Theodosius II. Lived 399 – 453 AD

CRS840: VF £400

EUDOCIA

Married Theodosius II in 421 AD, died 460 AD

CRS841: VF £400

From this point on all coins, unless otherwise stated are HALF SILIQUAE

VALENTINIAN III - 425 – 455 AD

CRS842: VF £300

CRS843: VF £300

CRS844: VF £300

CRS845: VF £350

CRS846: Siliqua **VF £400**

MARCIAN - 450 - 457 AD

CRS847: VF £300

CRS848: Siliqua **VF £400**
Seeming to continue a reverse of Theodosius II

The Roman Empire

LEO I - 457 – 474 AD

CRS849: VF £200

LIBIUS SEVERUS 461 – 465 AD
aka **SEVERUS III**

CRS850: VF £500

ZENO 474 – 490 AD

CRS851: VF £250

CRS852: VF £250

CRS853: VF £250

BASILISCUS 475 – 476 AD
Rebel against Zeno

CRS854: VF £400

Appendix I. Extra Notes by Coin Number

CRS2 Obv: Hercules was ordered by the gods to serve King Eurystheus for twelve years, after which he would become immortal. Eurystheus gave him a total of twelve very difficult tasks to perform - the first being to procure the skin of the monstrous Nemaean lion, which Hercules had to strangle with his bare hands. He is commonly shown on coins with the lion's skin either round his neck (as here), or over his head (e.g. CRS201). Here he also has his club over his shoulder. Rev. The wolf suckles Romulus and Remus. The King of Alba Longa feared the babies, and ordered them drowned in the River Tiber; but the king's servant placed them in a basket before depositing them in the river. They floated down to where the future Rome would be built - they were found by, and suckled by, a wolf. Romulus later founded Rome.

CRS9 (+ CRS15a) Rev: "Dioscuri" literally means "sons of Zeus (or Jupiter)". At the Battle of Lake Regillus against the Latins in 479BC the Romans were having a bad time. The Dioscuri suddenly rode in to support the Romans, and they won the battle.

CRS12 Rev: When the Romans or Greeks won a battle they commonly decorated the stump of a tree with arms and armour taken from fallen enemy. This was known as a "trophy".

CRS13 Diana, goddess of hunting, was also thought of as goddess of the moon, as here, where she wears a crescent on her head.

CRS14 Roma is seated on a pile of shields, with the "wolf and twins" to the right of her.

CRS15 Obv: Head of Apollo wearing a laurel-wreath (as he frequently does).
Rev: Jupiter in the quadriga wields his usual weapon, a thunderbolt.

CRS26 Oblong shields and a carnyx (trumpet) in saltire.

CRS111 Obv and Rev: Juno Sospita was protectress against the dangers of war. She wears the skin of a goat.

CRS113 Obv: Head considered to be that of Vercingetorix, with an oblong Gallic shield behind. He was a leader of the Gauls against Julius Caesar.

CRS116 Obv: Head of Bacchus, god of wine, wearing, as usual, a wreath of ivy.
Rev: Ceres, the corn-goddess holding two corn-ears. She is in a chariot pulled by two serpents.

CRS161 Obv: Head of Juno wearing a veil over the back part of her head. Juno was one of the three divinities of the Roman Capitol. The heads of the other two, Jupiter and Minerva, are also used as obverses of this type. Rev. Triumphal chariot with a small victory standing on top of it.

CRS162 King Aretas of Nabataea (Arabia) holds out an olive branch. He is submitting to the Romans.

CRS163 Two soldiers fighting, one with a whip, the other with a sword.

CRS164 Macedonian shield, with an elephant's head in centre.

CRS165-6 Monument to an ancestor who in 439BC reduced the price of corn in Rome.

CRS167 Horseman holds sword and head of a barbarian.

CRS168 The Dioscuri, each with a small star above head.

CRS171 The basket of Romulus and Remus came to rest by a fig tree, and later, the shepherd Faustulus (at the left) took the twins away from the wolf and brought them up.

CRS172 Hercules wrestles with the Nemaean lion.

CRS173 Obv: Bust of Virtus ("courage"). Rev: Manlius Aquillius raises up "Sicily".

CRS174 Cornucopia (Horn of plenty) on a globe, between sceptre and (on Rev) a rudder.

CRS175 Obv: The head may be that of Scipio Africanus the Elder. Rev: Jupiter between Juno and Minerva.

CRS176 Head of either Roma or Mars.

CRS177 Obv: Head of Mars. Rev: Two Gallic trumpets and two shields.

CRS178-9 Obv: Head of Mars.

CRS180 Head of Roma surrounded by a torque (collar). An ancestor of the moneyer had killed a gigantic Gaul in single combat, and taken from him his torque - this earned for his family the surname "Torquatus".

CRS181 In the Social War of 90-88BC Rome was opposed by the Marsic Federation of neighbouring Italian states. The obverse head is that of "Italia". The reverse shows two soldiers touching with their swords a pig held by the man who kneels in the centre. This was a Roman way of making an oath (see also CRS184). The legends are in the OSCAN script.

CRS182 Obv: Head of Janus. Rev: Roma builds a trophy (see note on CRS12).

CRS183 "Janiform" head of the Dioscuri.

CRS184 Obv: The Dei Penates, who were worshipped as gods of the household. Rev. soldiers swearing an oath over a sow (see note on CRS181 Rev)

CRS185 Obv: The heads of Numa Pompilius and Ancus Marcius, two early kings of Rome.

CRS186 Minted by Brutus (who later minted CRS301 - 306) as a young man in his capacity as one of the regular mint officials. The heads are those of ancestors.

CRS187 Obv: The moneyer's grandfather, of the same name, who was a consul.
Rev: Head of Sol the sun-god, who is always shown radiate.

CRS188 Rev: Head of "Sors" - a "sors" was an oracular response, often written on a tablet as the one below the half-figure.

CRS189 Obv: Head, or mask, of the Gorgon Medusa. Rev: Aurora (the "Dawn") leading out the four horses of the Sun, ready to harness them to the chariot which Apollo, the sun-god, was supposed to drive across the sky each day.

CRS190 Obv: The head of the gorgon Medusa is in the centre of the "triskelis" (three legs). The triskelis represents Sicily, where this coin was struck. Rev: Jupiter stands holding an eagle and a thunderbolt.

CRS191 Obv: Turreted head of the goddess Cybele. Rev: "Bacchius" is unknown to history, but may be another name for Judas Aristobulus II, a Jewish ruler who submitted to Pompey in 63BC.

CRS192-3 Rev: The sella curulis, "curule chair", the official seat used by leading Roman officials.

CRS193 Obv: Turreted head of "the City" Note that behind is a deformed foot.

CRS194 Obv: Head of King Philip V of Macedon, 220 - 179BC. Rev: Equestrian statue of L. Philippus, an ancestor of the moneyer, who concluded a treaty of friendship with Philip V.

CRS195 Obv: Head of Sol, the sun-god.

CRS196 Obv: Bust Of Mercury, the messenger of the gods, with his staff, the "caduceus", behind. Rev: Ulysses (Odysseus) returns to his island home of Ithaca after an absence of twenty years. As he does not know what to expect he is disguised; but his old dog Argus recognises him, wags his tail and then dies of old age.

CRS197 Obv: Head of Diana Planciana, wearing a "petasus". Rev: A quiver, a bow, and a goat.

CRS198-200 Obv: Head of Juno Sospita. See note on CRS111.

CRS199 Rev: At the yearly festival in honour of Juno Sospita held at Lanuvium, a maiden descended into the grotto under the temple to feed the serpent that lived there. If the girl was chaste she got out of the grotto safely afterwards!

CRS201 Obv: Head of Hercules. Rev: The savage Erymanthean boar which Hercules captured alive and carried on his shoulders to King Eurystheus (see note on CRS2).

CRS202 See note on CRS186. Obv: Head of "Liberty". Rev: The consul L. Junius Brutus (an ancestor) walking between two lictors with an usher in front.

CRS203-4 Obv: Head of Tatius, King of the Sabines, from whom the moneyer may have traced his descent.

CRS203 Rev: Tarpeia (in the centre), who betrayed a Roman fortress to the Sabines for gold. The Sabines were so disgusted by her treachery that they threw their shields down on her, so killing her.

CRS204 Rev: The "Rape of the Sabine women". The earliest Romans were all men. They tricked the Sabines by inciting them to compete in games - "and bring your ladies with you". At an appropriate moment each Roman snatched a Sabine girl and raced off back to Rome.

CRS205 Obv: Veiled head of "Concord". Rev: L Aemilius Paullus, who defeated and captured the Macedonian King Perseus in 168BC, raises up a trophy. At the left stand Perseus and his two sons as prisoners.

CRS206 Obv: Head of local Italian god Vejovis (who may have been equated with Jupiter) wielding a thunderbolt. Rev: The two Lares praestites, who were deities protecting the city of Rome.

CRS207 Obv: Uncertain male head. Rev: The Dioscuri

CRS208 Obv: Head of Apollo. Rev: The Dioscuri allowing their horses to drink.

CRS209 Obv: Head of Flora wearing a wreath of flowers. Rev: Two warriors.

CRS210 Obv: Head of Saturn. Rev: Two Quaestors seated - these were Roman officials, who were overseeing a law selling corn at a low price.

CRS211 Obv: Head of Apollo. Rev: Roma seated on shields being crowned by a Victory

CRS212 Obv: Head of "Piety". Rev: One of the Sicilian brothers carrying his father. The story is that the brothers saved their parents from an eruption of Mount Etna by carrying them to safety on their shoulders.

CRS213 Obv: Head of Venus. Rev: Three trophies (see note on CRS12).

CRS214 Obv: See note on CRS187 Obv: Rev. Figure seated on a sacrificial table between two trophies.

CRS215 Obv: Head of Hercules. Rev: Rider with two horses - in a certain race each jockey had to ride the course vaulting from one horse to another.

CRS216 Obv: Head of Ceres, goddess of corn. Rev: Man ploughing with two oxen.

CRS217 Rev: Two yoked oxen.

CRS218 Obv: Head of Diana, bow and quiver at back. Rev: Wild boar attacked by hound, spear in back.

CRS219 Obv: Head of Roma. Rev: Equestrian statue on triumphal arch.

CRS220 Obv: Head of Apollo.

CRS221 Obv: Head of Ancius Marcius, ancient king of Rome. Rev: Equestrian statue on an aqueduct.

CRS222 Obv: Head of Apollo.

CRS223 Obv: Head of Apollo, pickaxe behind. Rev: Valeria Luperca (ancestress of the moneyer) seated on a heifer.

CRS224 Obv: Head of Diana, bow and quiver at shoulder. Rev: Man standing on rocks, about to sacrifice an ox.

CRS225 Obv: Head of Vejovis, thunderbolt below (see note on CRS206 Obv.)
Rev: Winged genius on a goat. The caps of the Dioscuri above.

CRS226 Obv: Head of "Gaul", with carnyx (trumpet) behind. Rev: Diana of Ephesus holding a stag.

CRS227 Obv: Head of Neptune, trident behind. Rev: Winged genius on a dolphin.

CRS228 Obv: Head of Venus.

CRS229 Obv: Head of Hispania (Spain). Rev: Figure standing between Roman Legionary eagle and fasces (bundle of rods and an axe carried by lictors, as on CRS202)

CRS230	Obv: Head of "Piety" with stork in front.
CRS231	Obv: Head of Jupiter.
CRS232	Obv: Head of Apollo.
CRS233	Obv: Head of Diana. Rev. Hunting dog, with spear below.
CRS234	Obv: Head of a sibyl (prophetess). Rev. Sphinx,
CRS235	Obv: Head of Bacchus (see note on 116 Obv.) Rev. Pegasus.
CRS236	Obv: Head of Mutinius Titinus, who was especially worshipped by young married women.
CRS237	Obv: Head of Bonus Eventus, god of good fortune.
CRS238	Obv: Head of Vulcan, the blacksmith god, tongs behind.
CRS239	Obv: Head of Victory, with wings showing at her shoulders. Rev. Legionary eagle between two standards.
CRS240	Obv: Head of Venus or "Piety". Rev: Winged victory.
CRS241	Obv: Head of Roma.
CRS242	Obv: Head of Victory. Rev: Mars holding sword and trophy.
CRS243	Obv: Head of Apollo, lyre behind (he was god of music). Rev: Diana standing holding two torches.
CRS244	Obv: Head of Apollo. Rev: Marsyas with wine-skin over shoulder (he challenged Apollo to a musical contest - but lost).
CRS245	Obv: Head of Jupiter. Rev: Juno Sospita, with serpent in front (see note on CRS111).
CRS246	Obv: Head of Salus (means "Health"). Rev: Salus holding serpent and leaning against column.
CRS247	Obv: Head of Vesta. Rev: Man dropping tablet into voting-urn.
CRS248	Obv: Mask of Pan Rev: Jupiter Axurus seated.
CRS249	Obv: Head of Jupiter. Rev: Temple of Jupiter Capitolinus.
CRS250	Rev: Temple of Jupiter Capitolinus.
CRS251	Obv: Veiled head of Vesta. Rev: Curule chair within circular Temple of Vesta.
CRS252	Obv: Head of Venus Rev. The Acropolis of Eryx in Sicily, showing the Temple of Venus.
CRS253	Obv: Head of "Liberty". Rev: The "Rostrum" at Rome, on which is a magistrate's seat. The Rostrum was a curved set of arches decorated with ships' prows.
CRS254	Obv: Uncertain head (? Fortune). Rev: Pediment of temple.
CRS255	Obv: Head of Bonus Eventus ("Good Fortune"). Rev: Well-head upon which are two lyres.
CRS257	Obv: Head of Ceres. Rev: Curule chair between fasces (see notes on; CRS192 and CRS229 Rev.)
CRS258	Obv: Head of Apollo.
CRS258/9	258 Re. & 259 Obv & Rev, a Curule chair.
CRS260	Obv: Head of Fortune. Rev: Caduceus (the staff of Mercury) and palm.
CRS261	Obv: Head of? Bonus Eventus (good fortune). Rev: Caduceus.
CRS262	Obv: Head of "Piety".
CRS263	Obv: Head of "Concord".
CRS264	Obv: Head of Venus. Rev: Ear of corn, fasces and caduceus. (see note on CRS229 Rev)
CRS265	Obv: Head of a Sibyl (prophetess). Rev: Tripod surrounded by a torque (see note on CRS180)
CRS266	Obv: Head of Venus. Rev: Double cornucopiae (horns of plenty).

CRS267 Obv: Head of Juno Moneta (Juno the "giver of good counsel"). The mint was originally attached to her Temple: hence the use of "Moneta" for "money". Rev: Anvil with tongs and hammer. Vulcan's domed cap above.

CRS268 Obv: Genius of the Roman People, sceptre over shoulder. Rev: Globe between sceptre and rudder.

CRS269 Obv: Veiled head of Vesta. Rev: Knife, simpulum (cup used for religious ceremonies) and ornamental axe.

CRS270 Obv: Head of "Piety". Rev: jug and Lituus (the special staff of an augur - an augur was a soothsayer).

CRS271 Obv: Head of a consul ancestor of the moneyer

CRS273-4 Obv: Head of Apollo wearing laurel wreath. Rev. Victory with a trophy.

CRS275 Obv: Head of Jupiter laureate.

CRS279 Obv: Head of Apollo. Rev: Winged victory.

CRS280 Obv: Head of Victory, wing visible at shoulder. Rev: Woman feeding serpent.

CRS281 Obv: Head of Neptune, trident at shoulder. Rev: Snake round altar in front of Victory.

CRS282 Obv: Head of Victory. Rev: Pegasus.

CRS283 Obv: Head of ?Bacchus wearing ivy-wreath. Rev: Victory seated.

CRS284 Obv: Head of Venus. Rev: Cupid walking,

CRS285 Smaller version of CRS222

CRS286 Obv: Bust of Jupiter.

CRS287 Obv: Bust of Numa Pompilius, an early King of Rome.

CRS288 Obv: Head of Roma. Rev: "Hispania" (Spain) presenting palm to Pompey, who is stepping off a galley.

CRS289 Obv: Head of Pompey the Great. Rev: Neptune between the Sicilian brothers (see CRS212 note).

CRS290 Obv: Head of Neptune. Rev: A naval "trophy" (see CRS12 note).

CRS291 Obv: The lighthouse at Messana (the modern Messina), with a galley in front. Rev: The sea-monster Scylla.

CRS292 Obv: Elephant trampling on serpent. Rev: Sacrificial implements (see CRS269), simpulum, sprinkler, axe, and "apex" (priest's hat).

CRS293 Obv: Head of Venus. Rev: Aeneas escaping from Troy, carrying his father, and the "palladium" (a statue of Minerva).

CRS294 Obv: Head of Venus. Rev: Sacrificial implements.

CRS295 Obv: Head of Venus. Rev: A trophy and captives.

CRS296 Obv: Veiled head of Caesar, with apex behind - veiled for him to act as a priest.

CRS297 Obv: Head of Caesar. Rev: Venus standing.

CRS299-300 Obv: Head on these two coins may represent a personification of "the New Age" rather than Julius Caesar!

CRS300 Obv: Head of Caesar with comet above (a comet appeared shortly after Caesar's death). Rev: A priest standing.

CRS301 Obv: Head of Apollo. Rev: A trophy (see CRS12 note).

CRS302 Obv & Rev: Sacrificial implements.

CRS303 Obv: Head of "Liberty".

CRS304 Obv: Head of Brutus. Rev: "The Ides of March" (the day Brutus participated in the assassination of Caesar) "Cap of Liberty" between two daggers.

CRS305 Obv: Magisterial stool. Rev: Tripod.

CRS306 Obv: Head of "Liberty". Rev: Anchor and prow of galley.

CRS307 Obv: Head of "Liberty". Rev: Jug and Lituus (see CRS270 note).

CRS308	Obv & Rev: "sacrificial implements" and raven.
CRS309	Rev: Radiate head of "Sol" in temple.
CRS310	Obv: Mark Antony dressed as a priest. Rev: Head of Sol (the sun-god).
CRS312	Rev: Legionary eagle between two standards.
CRS314-5	Rev: Lion.
CRS316	Rev: Head of Octavia on "cista mystica" (special chest connected with the worship of Bacchus, god of wine), with entwined serpents.
CRS320-1	Rev: Caduceus (see CRS260 note).
CRS322	Obv: Head of Mars. Rev: Trophy above legionary eagle between two standards.
CRS324	Rev: Thunderbolt.
CRS325	Rev: Statue of Caesar in temple dedicated to "the divine Julius". Altar at left.
CRS327-9	Obv: Bust of Venus.
CRS328	Obv: Head of Feronia. Rev: Kneeling Parthian handing back a Roman standard.
CRS329	Obv: Eagle, consular robes (the shell-like object) and a wreath. Rev: A triumphal chariot.
CRS332	Capricorn, with cornucopia on back, holding globe & rudder.
CRS333	Minted 28BC, recording the conquest of Egypt after the deaths of Antony & Cleopatra.
CRS334	Rev: Shield between two laurel trees.
CRS335	Altar dedicated to "Fortuna".
CRS336	Rev: Apollo holding lyre and plectrum.
CRS338	Rev: The round temple of Mars the Avenger.
CRS339	Rev: A comet (see CRS300 note).
CRS340	Rev: An oak-wreath presented to Augustus by grateful citizens.
CRS341	Rev: The "golden shield of valour" presented to Augustus.
CRS342	Rev: Caius & Lucius Caesar standing facing, shields and spears between. Simpulum (see CRS269 note) and Lituus above.
CRS344	Rev: Capricorn with cornucopia (Augustus was conceived in the Zodiacal sign of Capricorn).
CRS345	Rev: Victory crowning a trophy.
CRS346	See CRS316 for type, victory on cista mystica.
CRS347	When an Emperor died he was usually "deified" - hence DIVO (or DIVVS) before a name means that the person referred to is dead. Rev: An altar.
CRS349	Rev: Livia, Tiberius' mother, seated as "Pax", holding olive branch.
CRS350	Tiberius in a quadriga.
CRS351+5	Rev: An oak-wreath presented to Augustus by grateful citizens.
CRS356	Rev: "Nemesis" preceded by a serpent. There were two Nemeses, winged female figures shown plucking their dresses at the neck. These measured out happiness and unhappiness for mortals.
CRS357	Rev: A praetorian camp, within which a soldier and a legionary eagle.
CRS358	A triumphal arch commemorating Claudius' conquest of Britain.
CRS359	"Fortune" crowning Claudius.
CRS360	Rev: Claudius in a quadriga.
CRS361	Rev: Cart with winged victories on top and on sides.
CRS362	Rev: legend on shield, behind which is a spear.
CRS363	Sacrificial implements.
CRS364	Ceres, the corn goddess, holding long torch, and poppy-seed and corn-ears.

CRS365	Rev: Nero, radiate, holding laurel-branch and victory.
CRS371	Rev: Candelabrum.
CRS374	Rev: Two lighted torches joined by a garland.
CRS379	Livia standing.
CRS387	Dolphin above tripod, in which is a raven.
CRS394	Rev: Vesta seated holding a lighted torch.
CRS396	Jupiter standing.
CRS400	Commemorating the subjection of Judaea after the Jewish revolt of 66 - 70AD. "Judaea" seated mourning below a trophy.
CRS404	A lighted altar.
CRS406	Neptune holding sceptre and aplustre (curved ornament at stern of ship).
CRS410	A throne.
CRS413	Rev: Venus holding helmet and spear.
CRS415	Wolf and twins (see CRS2 note). In exergue, a boat.
CRS416	Helmet on throne.
CRS417	A lighted altar.
CRS418-9	Minerva.
CRS423	Rev: Peacock.
CRS424	Baby boy seated on globe, surrounded by seven stars.
CRS428	Sacrificial implements.
CRS431	Mars carrying spear and trophy.
CRS432	"Piety" pouring libation at an altar.
CRS433	"Eternity" holding the heads of the Sun and the Moon.
CRS435	The "River Danube" reclining.
CRS436	Trajan's father seated on a curule chair holding patera (Saucer) and sceptre.
CRS441	Rev: Vesta holding Palladium (see 293 note) and sceptre.
CRS443	Rev: Matidia as "Piety" looking after two children.
CRS445	"Adoption" - Trajan, who adopted Hadrian. Shown greeting his new son.
CRS446	"Egypt" reclining. She holds a sistrum (used in the worship of Isis). At left, an ibis.
CRS462	"ANNONA" (the Grain supply) holding corn ears in her right hand. Her left hand rests on a modius (a sort of bucket for measuring out grain). The modius is on the prow of a galley.
CRS467	Modius (see CRS462 note) with corn and poppy-seed.
CRS470	Funeral pyre of four tiers, with quadriga on top.
CRS471	Statue of Antoninus Pius on a column.
CRS477	"Virtus" (Courage) holding spear and parazonium.
CRS479	Mars.
CRS480	"Providentia" holding sceptre and a wand over globe.
CRS482	"Roma" seated on a pile of arms.
CRS487	Venus holds an apple, and a rudder placed on a dove.
CRS490	Diana "the Light bearer", holding a long torch.
CRS491	Juno holding patera (saucer used for pouring libations) and sceptre. Peacock to left.
CRS492	Draped throne on which are two baby boys.

CRS495	Throne with sceptre lying across it. Peacock in front.
CRS498	"Parthia" seated on the ground as a captive. Quiver, bow, and shield to right.
CRS506	"Liberty" holding Sceptre and cap of liberty.
CRS507	"Piety" seated with child in front of her.
CRS508	Jupiter at right placing hand on shoulder of Commodus
CRS509	Commodus on platform addressing three soldiers with standards.
CRS510	Commodus considered himself to be a reincarnation of Hercules!
CRS524	Minerva the Peace-bearer.
CRS526	The Sun-god holding a whip (to drive the chariot of the sun across the sky).
CRS528	A trophy with two captives.
CRS532	Dea Caelestis (Cybele) riding on a lion.
CRS537	Funeral pyre of four tiers with a quadriga on top.
CRS544	Hercules standing.
CRS545	Mars with spear and trophy.
CRS546	Minerva and a trophy.
CRS547	Lion with a thunderbolt in its mouth.
CRS548	Head of Sol, the sun-god.
CRS552	Serapis, modius on head, raising right hand and holding sceptre.
CRS554	Genius holding patera over altar and two corn-ears.
CRS557	"Felicitas" (Prosperity) holding cornucopia and caduceus.
CRS558	"Fides exercitus" (the Faith of the Army). Fides with legionary standards.
CRS559	"Fortuna Redux" (Returning good fortune).
CRS560	Jupiter the Protector. The small figure of Macrinus under his arm.
CRS561	"Annona" (the grain-supply) (see CRS462 note)
CRS563	Diadumenian with military standards.
CRS568	The sun-god (see CRS526 note).
CRS569	The sacred stone of the Syrian sun-god Elagabal being carried in a triumphal car.
CRS570-1	Elagabalus had been a priest of Elagabal at Emisa in Syria, He is shown here as a priest at an altar.
CRS575	"Spes" (Hope) holding flower, and raising dress.
CRS576	"Pax" (Peace) standing.
CRS579	Jupiter the Avenger.
CRS581	Altar.
CRS586	Cybele, "the mother of the gods", with lions crouching by her throne.
CRS589	The Moon, the "light-bearer" riding in a biga.
CRS593	Plautilla and Caracalla standing hand in hand.
CRS598	"Pudicitia" (Chastity) pulling at her veil.
CRS599	"Fecunditas" (Fertility) holding a cornucopia, with a child at her feet.
CRS602	Julia Maesa being carried up to heaven on a peacock.
CRS612	"Victory in Germany". Winged victory and German captive.
CRS614	Julia Maesa being carried up to heaven on a peacock.
CRS615	"Leader of the young men". Maximus with two military standards.
CRS618	VICTORIA AVGG "The victory of the Augusti" - the double-G of AVGG means that there are two Emperors referred to.

CRS631 The sun-god standing.

CRS637 In 248AD the Romans celebrated the 1000th anniversary of the city - this was commemorated with lavish public games, etc; and these were known as the "Secular Games" - thus SAEGULARES AUGG on the coins.

CRS650 Philip I and Philip II seated on curule chairs.

CRS657 Pannonia was an area of Central Europe in the area of the modern Austria and Croatia. It had been divided by the Romans into Upper Pannonia and lower Pannonia - hence the plural PANNONIAE.

CRS687-9 Valerian is "Restorer of the world", "Restorer of the East", and "Restorer of the Human Race".

CRS695 When Jupiter was born he had to be hidden away in Crete to avoid his being eaten by his father Saturn. He was brought up by a goat. IOVI CRESCENTI means "the growing Jupiter".

CRS696 VICTORIA PART "Parthian Victory". Victory presenting a wreath to Valerian II.

CRS697 An eagle carrying Valerian II to heaven.

CRS703 "Spes" (Hope) on the right presenting a flower to Saloninus.

CRS707 A griffin "sacred to Apollo"

CRS708 Commemorating victories by Gallienus over the Germans.

CRS709 A "Legionary" coin. "Legio Prima Adiutrix".

CRS713 A goat "sacred to Juno".

CRS714 Serapis standing.

CRS718 This type, with the obverse showing Postumus holding the club of Hercules over his shoulder repeats the reverse of Commodus (CRS510).

CRS722 Neptune reclining holding a trident and an anchor.

CRS723 "Britannia" holding a trident greets Carausius at the right.

CRS725-7 The four Tetrarchs (Diocletian, Maximianus, Constantius and Galerius) sacrifice over a tripod outside a city gate.

CRS731 "Africa" holding a military standard and an elephant tusk.

CRS742 "Jupiter the Protector of the Emperor". Jupiter holding sceptre and thunderbolt, riding on an eagle.

CRS758 The VOTIS coins. An Emperor made vows for so many years of his reign, and then made more for a subsequent period. On CRS758 VOTIS XX means that he has fulfilled his vows for a period of 20 years: MVLT XXX, that he has undertaken renewed vows for the next ten years to bring him up to 30 in all. Unfortunately the "VOTIS" period was often contracted because celebrations could begin early - so VOTIS XX could mean that Constantius II had reigned for 19 years, and the coin type could continue for some time thereafter.

CRS766 "The courage of the army" - Latin is changing. Classical usage would have written the genitive of "army" as EXERCITUS (as CRS636).

CRS778 Rev: "The Restorer of the world". Valentinian holding small Victory and the "Labarum", the Christian standard with the Christian monogram ☧.

CRS796 Rev: The phoenix, symbol of immortality, standing on a globe.

CRS798 "The courage of the Romans".

CRS835 Rev: The "Christogram", the first two letters of "Christos" in Greek put into the form of a monogram.

Appendix II. The Names and Titles

Title	Notes
Lf, Mf, etc	"filius" - "Son of", following the forename of the father. Thus Lf = "son of Lucius" Mf = "son of Marcus".
III VIR RFC	Member of the "Triumvirate for the establishment of the Republic", one of three leaders who divided the power of the state between them - the most notable Triumvirate being that of Antony, Lepidus and Octavian.
COS	Consul, often followed by a numeral, e.g. COS III, "Consul on three occasions".
COS DES (or DESIG)	Elected to the Consulate, but not yet in office. See CRS326, COS ITER ET TER DESIG "Consul twice, and elected to a third term of office".
CAESAR	Began as a personal family name but because it was the family name of Julius Caesar it was used as a name by all later Emperors. During the middle and later Empire it came to refer to a junior partner, or "Prince".
NC or NOB CAES, etc.	"Most noble Caesar" used as a title by Princes of the later Empire. See Appendix IIII.
AUGUSTUS	A title given to Octavian personally, but used by all later Emperors. During the middle and later Empire it came to refer to the Emperor (or partner Emperors) as opposed to the junior "Caesar". It is usually contracted to AUG. See also Appendix IIII.
IMPERATOR (IMP)	Originally referring to an occasion after a victory when the soldiers acclaimed their general as "imperator" - so in the earlier period there is often a numeral after IMP. Thus CRS409 gives Titus the title IMP XIIII, meaning that his troops had acclaimed him of fourteen occasions. Later it came to be just another title of the Emperor.
TR P or TRIB POT	This was the "Tribunician Power" which appears to have been the real legal basis of the power of an Emperor. As this was renewed annually (or more frequently) it gives the actual date of a coin - thus Septimius Severus was TR P in 193AD, TR P II in 194AD, TR P III in 195AD, etc. Unfortunately Emperors sometimes begin their TRIB POTs "early", as with Marcus Aurelius who began in 147AD.
PM	"Pontifex Maximus", "High Priest".
PP	"Pater Patriae", "Father of his country".
PF	"Pius, Felix", "Pious and blessed".
PRINCIPI IUVENTUTIS	"Leader of the young men", a title used by the Caesars.
DN	"Dominus noster", "Our Lord", used by later Emperors.
DIVUS of DIVO	"Deified", used of Emperors who had died.

Appendix III. Grading Roman Coins – A Rough Guide

The easiest way to determine condition is where there is a portrait.

A well struck coin in Very Fine (VF) condition must show most of the hair, though a small worn patch on the high point is allowable.

In Fine condition one would expect the clear outline of a head with some hair visible.

The legend may be partially off the coin because of the striking, or it may have suffered because of a worn die; but normally one would expect a coin in Very Fine condition to be clearly legible and most of a Fine coin to be more or less readable.

With ancient coins so many other factors can be involved such as toning, a coin being off-centre, having a ragged flan, or a crack, or signs of corrosion. Or a coin may appear worn on one side only because a worn die has been used for that side.

But, other factors apart, a coin in VF condition would normally be worth three times as much as one in Fine condition - or more! In the case of a Nero Sestertius, perhaps six times as much.

Appendix IIII. A short note on the "Ranks" of Caesar and Augustus

In the earliest days of the Empire the Emperor included both Caesar and Augustus in his own personal titles, but it soon became the custom to give the title "Caesar" to a "second-in-command", and to use "Augustus" as the title of the top man, or of equal ranking top men.

There could be several Caesars and Augusti at the same time, and it will help to note how this can be shown on coins. For example, "the Victory of the Emperor" can be written as VICTORIA AVG; but where there is more than one reigning Emperor this can be shown by adding extra G's - Victoria AVGG means "the Victory of the two Emperors", and VICTORIA AVGGG "the Victory of the three Emperors".

Appendix V. Mint cities, mid 3rd Century onwards.

On later Roman coins a mint signature will usually be found in the exergue at the bottom of the reverse. Mint-marks begin around the mid 3rd century AD; but come into full use from the time of Diocletian onwards. They consist of an abbreviation of the name of the mint, sometimes preceded by the letters SM (sacred mint), plus usually a variable letter to indicate which workshop at that mint minted any particular coin - as this letter is variable I show it below in italics. Here are some of the mints and mint-marks:

LONDON: *p*LN, *p*LON
TREVERI: (Rhineland) SMTR, *p*TR, TR*p*
LUGDUNUM: (Lyons) *p*LG LVG*p*
ARELATE/CONSTANTINA: (Arles, Southern France). Known between 328 and 340 AD as Constantina. Changed to Arelate in 340 AD, and then back to Constantina in 353 AD. *p*ARL ARL*a* *p*CONST *p*CON
TICINUM: (Northern Italy) *p*T
ROME: R*p* SMR*p*
AQUILEIA: (Northern Italy) AQ*p* SMAQ*p*
OSTIA: (near Rome) MOST*p*
SISCIA: (Croatia) *a*SIS SISC
SIRMIUM: (Serbia) *a*SIRM
THESSALONIKA: (Northern Greece) SMTS*a* TES*a* TS*a*
HERACLEA: (Turkey in Europe, near Constantinople) SMH*a* HERACLA
CONSTANTINOPLE: CONSa CONS
NICOMEDIA: (Asiatic Turkey, near Constantinople) SMN*a* MN*a*
CYZICUS: (Asiatic Turkey, near Constantinople) SMK*a*
ANTIOCH: (Turkey, near the Syrian border) SMANT*a* AN*a* ANT*a*
ALEXANDRIA: (Egypt) SMAL*a* ALE*a*
BARCINO: (Barcelona, Spain) SMB*a*
RAVENNA: (Northern Italy) RV RVPS
MEDIOLANUM: (Milan, Italy) MD MDPS MED

Appendix VI. Cleaning tips for Silver Roman Coins

The guidance below is offered to people who have purchased uncleaned, or have freshly dug up Roman coins. It is provided as guidance, and it should be borne in mind that some coins will always be harder to clean than others. Some will probably be impossible. If patience is not exercised when attempting to clean Roman coins, damage to the coin can result, so for this reason, lots of practice on cheap coins is recommended.

Be gentle with your coins; more coins are ruined by over zealous cleaning than anything else! For the cleaning of all ancient coins, you'll probably find the following useful: toothpicks, toothbrushes, soap, water, and lots of patience! For cleaning in between letters, toothpicks work great. For the more experienced collector, dental picks can also be useful, but these run the risk of scratching the coin and/or it's patina. Often, soft brass-brushes are needed, but as silver is more stable than copper based alloys this is usually not the case.

Silvered Coins

Silvered coins are mainly base metal, so cannot be cleaned using the methods for silver coins of good fineness. Generally soap, water and a toothbrush is the only way to clean silvered and silver-plated coins, without damaging the silver. The use of brass brushes or anything harsher will probably result in the silver layer being removed.

Silver Coins of Good fineness

Lemon Juice – Readily available, and it works very well on hard to clean silver coins. Soak the coin in the juice until the desired amount of crud has been removed. Give the coin a quick scrub every so often, and rinse it with fresh water to check the progress.

Ammonium - Will clean the coin without doing any damage to the silver, but it isn't as readily available as lemon juice.